THE SUNDAY TIMES
Guide to the Internet

Matthew Wall

HarperCollins

Matthew Wall is a freelance journalist and author best-known for his weekly *Web Wise* internet column in *The Sunday Times*. He also writes internet features for the paper's Doors section and has written several internet reports for business. He also advises companies on web design and strategy.

HarperCollins Publishers
Westerhill Rd
Bishopbriggs
Glasgow G64 2QT

www.collins.co.uk

First published 2000
Revised and Updated 2002

Reprint 10 9 8 7 6 5 4 3 2 1 0

ISBN 0 00 7126603

Printed and bound in Great Britain by
Clays Ltd, St. Ives plc

Acknowledgments

I would like to thank my wife, Wendy, for her patience
and encouragement during the writing of this book.
She kept the coffee flowing and confiscated my games disks
– essential interventions for which I am truly grateful. I would
also like to thank Christopher Riches and James Carney at
HarperCollins for their support and encouragement.

Contents

Part *1*

Getting Online

Chapter 1

Getting Started

Introduction

Welcome to the *Sunday Times Guide to the Internet.* This book tells you everything you need to know to get started on the internet – in plain English. It filters out all the stuff you don't need to know and concentrates on making the internet work for you, as simply and straightforwardly as possible.

If you've been put off by the internet's geeky reputation, intimidating technology and ludicrous jargon, then this book can help. It reduces the internet to what it really is: a very useful – but sometimes maddeningly frustrating – tool, which can also be great fun.

We've divided this guide into two parts. The first part tells you the basics – what type of equipment and software you need to get online; how to search and browse the internet efficiently; and how to use e-mail and download useful programs. The second part tells you how to make the most of the internet, whether you want to book a holiday, find the best online bank account, design your own website or simply find things out. As well as selecting the best websites for you to visit we also pay special attention to safety and security online. To put it simply, the *Sunday Times Guide to the Internet* is all you need.

So what's so great about the internet?

- You can write letters and send documents, pictures and sound files across the globe for the price of a local call using electronic mail (*e-mail* – see the Glossary on p. 275 for an explanation of *these* terms).

- You can shop online, book tickets and holidays, and manage your finances from the comfort of your own home, saving time and money in the process.

- You can swap views and ideas with like-minded people from all over the world via internet chat rooms, newsgroups and e-mail.

- You can find things out quickly and efficiently using *search engines* and directories.

- You can hear and read up-to-the-second news reports.

- You can *download* music and computer software on to your computer.

- You can play games simultaneously with other people who may even be in a different country.

- It never closes (except when your computer crashes!).

What is it exactly and how does it work?

Who cares? Do you really know how your microwave or mobile phone works? The internet is getting so widespread these days – there are over 500 million people online across the world – that it is no longer just a technical novelty beloved of enthusiasts. It is a mass-market means of communication, just like the television. And the amazing thing about the internet is how quickly it has managed to achieve this level of acceptance. It is hard to believe that a decade ago the internet barely registered in the public consciousness.

The Sunday Times website: top stories just a mouse click away (www.sunday-times.co.uk).

Anyway, if you really must know, the internet is basically lots of computers linked up to form networks sending and receiving digital data that can be still or animated images, video or sound. Pretty much anything can be translated into digital data (strings of ones and noughts), then chopped up into small parcels of information called 'packets', and sent across the telephone network. We receive television pictures through an aerial, satellite dish or cable connection, and the same goes for internet data.

The main way people access the internet is through computers linked up to the telephone network, at home and at work. But other ways of accessing the internet are rapidly being introduced. Interactive digital television, introduced to the UK in 1999, brought internet access into the living room, and the recent rise of internet-enabled mobile phones and hand-held organisers took it into the street. In fact, we're moving towards an 'internet anywhere' world in which even photo booths, telephone kiosks and bank cash machines are being equipped with internet access facilities. Don't be surprised if you find yourself surfing the net via your voice-activated in-car computer within the next year or two!

One point to make clear is that the **World Wide Web** is only one part of the internet, although it has rapidly become the most important and fastest-growing part.

What do I need to get started?

The basic requirements to get the most out of the internet are:

- a computer
- a **modem** (could be inside a digital TV set-top box)
- an internet service provider.

How do I choose the right computer?

Reading computer adverts is like entering a different universe inhabited by people who only talk in acronyms and abbreviations. There are so many variables. The problem with computers is that they are developing so fast. No sooner

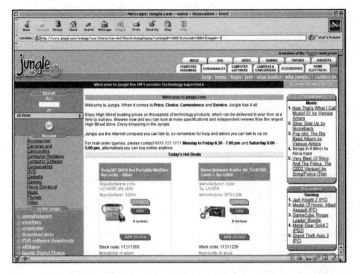

If you have access to the internet through work or a friend, you can purchase your own computer through websites such as the popular retailer, jungle.com.

have we splashed out on the latest model than it has been superseded by a faster one equipped with all the latest gizmos. The whole weight of the industry's marketing muscle is used to pressure us into upgrading even when we may not need to.

The fact is that these days you can buy a perfectly adequate internet-ready desktop computer for around £500, and prices are continuing to fall as competition amongst computer chip manufacturers intensifies. Yes, you can pay a lot more, but often that's for functions and power far beyond your requirements.

There are three main considerations when buying a PC: price, performance and service. The first thing to ask yourself

> ## TIP
>
> *When buying a computer, the first thing to ask yourself is what you want it for. If it is for simple word processing tasks and to send e-mail, you won't need a hugely powerful machine.*

is what you want the PC for. If it is to carry out simple word processing tasks and send e-mails, you're not going to need as powerful a machine as the games enthusiast.

There's also little point in going for a special deal that includes a scanner if you are never likely to use it. So don't get carried away by marketing hype. You don't need a Ferrari to go to the supermarket.

Mac or PC?

The first choice is between an Apple Macintosh (Mac) computer or what's called an IBM-compatible PC using Microsoft Windows or Microsoft NT as its operating system. Microsoft certainly dominates the market with a 90% market share. But those who use a Mac are a fanatical bunch who swear by its superior design and ease of use.

Apple Macs: for people who believe design matters

Generally speaking, Macs tend to be preferred by graphic designers and arty people. Certainly, if the look of your computer is important, the Macs beat the boring cream box PC hands down. But if compatibility with everything that's available on the web is more important, you may be better off sticking with the undisputed market leader.

Having said that, the main elements of both types of computer are the same:

The processor

This is the microchip brain of the PC. Its speed is measured in megahertz (MHz). The larger the number, the faster the machine. These days new machines come with a 700MHz chip as a bare minimum, and as the two main manufacturers, Intel and AMD compete furiously with each other, we're already seeing 2.2 GHz machines coming onto the market. However, some critics believe that the proportionate increase in speed is not high enough to justify continuous upgrades of your computer. But you do need at least 500MHz to cope with all the most modern applications.

Memory

The more Random Access Memory (RAM) a PC has, the more tasks it can carry out at the same time. If you don't have enough RAM, your PC can start to run slowly if you have many programs open at the same time. Around 128 megabytes (MB) is considered enough to handle most tasks required of a home PC, although highly specified PCs come with 256MB of RAM as standard. If speed is important to you, pay a bit extra for more RAM. A lot of PC retailers allow you to specify how much RAM you want in your machine.

Hard disk capacity

These days the storage capacity of PCs is measured in **gigabytes** – 1 gigabyte (GB) = 1,000MB. You need a large amount of space to store all the software programs you want to run and any documents, videos, pictures and sound files you choose to keep. Around 10GB is considered the bare minimum these days. Most well-equipped PCs will have around 20-40GB.

Modem

The good news is that almost all new PCs now come with a modem built in, so it's just a question of plugging your PC into the telephone socket to get online. The modem is a gadget that converts digital data into analogue format for transmission across the telephone network and vice versa for incoming data. Modem speed is measured in kilobits per second (kbps). The standard speed is now 56kbps – the higher the number, the faster you can send e-mails and download web pages. Just make sure the modem is 'V.90 compliant'. This means that the modem is capable of talking to all the different makes and models of modem that exist on the market.

If you already have a computer that doesn't have an internal modem you need to buy an external one and plug it into the back of your computer. There are lots on the market, some offering fax and answering machine facilities, too. Go for the fastest and make sure it's V.90 compliant.

If you want to connect using a laptop or notebook computer, the newest models also come with modems built in. Otherwise, there is a whole range of credit-card sized 'PCMCIA' modems on the market that simply slot in at the side of the computer. Some just enable you to connect to the internet via the normal telephone network. Others also allow you to connect using your mobile phone, or link up to your company's computer system.

There are other ways of connecting much faster to the internet – using **ISDN** lines, **cable modems** or **ADSL** technology – but these are dealt with in *Faster Surfing, pages 77–89.*

Screen size

It can be quite annoying viewing web pages designed for a large monitor on one that is too small. As PC use has become visually richer, screen size and quality have become more important. Basically, the larger the screen the better. Most good PCs will be a minimum of 15 inches measured diagonally from corner to corner, but you can go up to 19 inches or more.

Graphics

If you're interested in playing games on your PC, you'll need a PC with a powerful graphics card capable of handling the very latest, visually rich games that are on the market. Look for the amount of memory the card has – 32MB is ideal.

Software

To make their PCs more attractive, manufacturers and retailers will often include software packages – programs that perform specific tasks – with the PC. But just because a PC may come with the various versions of Windows operating system pre-loaded, don't assume that it will come with all the other software you'll need, too. The operating system software isn't the same as the word processing or spreadsheet software, for example. This is a common misconception. Buying software separately can add several hundred pounds to the overall cost of the PC, so look very carefully at what's included in the price.

Service

The quality of after-sales service is almost as important as the specification of the PC itself. All machines are fallible. In fact, it seems that the more powerful and complicated PCs become, the more likely it is that something will go wrong. Often, glitches are nothing to do with the computer hardware, but with the software that came with it.

Software designers are constantly bringing out revised versions of their programs, and Microsoft is no exception. Its latest operating system, Windows XP, is rapidly superseding earlier versions.

WARNING

Look closely at the quality of the telephone support offered by an ISP. Home users are more likely to use PCs after work, so a helpline that shuts at 5pm is not much use.
Ideally, you want free, 24-hour lifetime support.

If something does go wrong with your machine, the last thing you want is to have to send it back to the retailer or manufacturer. An 'on-site' warranty, where an engineer will come to your home and mend your PC for you, is best. 'Pick-up-and-return' warranties are also useful. Most manufacturers' warranties last for just one year, although you can sometimes pay extra to extend the period.

What is an internet service provider?

An internet service provider (**ISP**) is a company that acts as a gateway to the internet. All data coming to and from your computer goes through the ISP first. For example, when people send you e-mail they don't send it direct to your computer. It goes first to your ISP's computers (known as servers) and sits there until you request it. The mail is then sent to your computer.

ISPs can offer several e-mail addresses, free space to create your own web pages, entertainment, shopping and information services, plus technical support. But the best thing about ISPs is that you connect to them at local call rates, even if you're sending an e-mail to California or downloading web pages from Australia. More are offering unmetered calls for a fixed monthly fee.

Most ISPs used to charge a monthly fee of around £10 to £15 for access to the internet. But this way of charging was blown out of the water by Freeserve, a free ISP service launched in 1998 by Dixons, the electrical retailer. Nearly everyone has followed suit.

So how do I choose one?

Choosing an ISP depends largely on how you plan to use the internet. Here's a checklist of topics to consider – some may be more important to you than others.

Technical support

This is very important. If you're new to the internet you're likely to need quite a bit of help, especially if there are gremlins in the ISP's software, as there sometimes are. You need to find an ISP with a support line that stays open as long as possible, or at least during the hours when you're

19

most likely to be online. Ideally, look for 24-hour, seven-day-a-week help. But watch out for the cost. Many of these 'free' ISPs charge 50p to £1 a minute and some don't offer any help at all.

Free web space

Many ISPs offer you free space on their servers so that you can design your own web pages. If you fancy doing this, and airing your family photos, doodles, poems and hobbies in public, look for an ISP that offers the most megabytes of web space. The more sophisticated you want to make your website, the more memory you'll need. Around 10MB to 25MB should be enough. Some ISPs offer unlimited space.

> **TIP**
>
> When choosing an Internet Service Provider, look in specialist internet magazines for tests that show which are the fastest and most reliable.

Multiple e-mail addresses

If other members of your family use the PC, look for an ISP that offers several e-mail addresses. That way your private e-mail won't be read by anyone else.

Speed and reliability

The internet is a vast network of computers and as such is only as fast as the weakest link in the chain. Some ISPs are faster and more reliable than others, and if you plan to use the internet extensively, this matters. It can be pretty annoying if you're expecting an important e-mail and you can't access it because your ISP's systems have crashed, or you have to wait ages for web pages to download because your ISP doesn't have enough servers or modems to handle demand.

Specialist internet magazines carry out exhaustive tests on all the leading ISPs, checking them for speed and reliability. A free ISP isn't necessarily less reliable, although, on average, the ISPs that still charge a monthly fee come out best. If reliability is your number one priority, it still may be worth paying for your internet access.

ISP services

Some ISPs offer their members entertainment, shopping and information services (known as 'content' in the jargon) that aren't available to non-members. You have to subscribe and load their software on to your computer. The most popular of these so-called 'proprietary' ISPs are America On-Line (AOL) and CompuServe. If you want to check out their services before committing yourself to a monthly fee, you can usually find their software on free CD-ROMs attached to the front of internet magazines. Bear in mind that free ISPs, such as FreeServe and Virgin Net, also offer their own content on their websites, making it available to members and non-members alike.

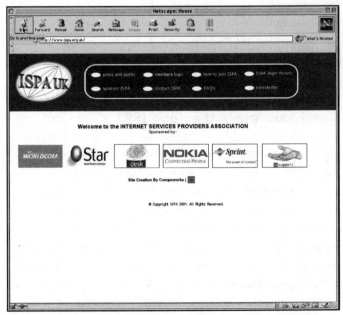

You can find a full list of ISPA members on its web site (www.ispa.org.uk).

Is a particular ISP a member of the Internet Services Providers Association (ISPA)?

It is not essential for your ISP to be a member of the ISPA (**www.ispa.org.uk**), but its members do agree to stick to a code of conduct and there is a standardised complaints procedure if you're unhappy with your ISP's level of service.

What if I'm a Mac user?

The brutal fact is that computer life is dominated by Microsoft in almost every area. Until the breakthrough introduction of the iMac it wasn't easy to get online with a Mac at all. Even though there has been a vast improvement, many ISPs are still not geared up to give technical support to Mac users. Many websites are not designed to be used by Macs. Before you sign up with an ISP, check that they are fully Mac-friendly. Once online, there are plenty of Mac-related websites to help you navigate the net in a way most suitable for your machine. Try these for starters:

www.apple.com
www.macobserver.com
www.macuser.co.uk
www.everymac.com

Can I have more than one ISP?

There's nothing to stop you having links to several ISPs on your computer. In fact it can be a good idea to have a back-up connection if one breaks down for some reason. It can also be practical to have one e-mail address for business and one for personal use. If you've set up your e-mail address with one ISP you can even access your mail using another ISP. The only thing you can't do is *send* e-mail from a competing ISP.

More often than not new computers will come with software for one or two ISPs already loaded. You don't have to use them if you don't want to, but there's no reason to get rid of them either. They can be useful for back-up.

Do I need to install a new telephone line to get online?

No, but it is a good idea if you can afford it. As the internet uses the telephone system, anyone trying to ring you will just get an engaged tone if you're online. Surfing the internet can become addictive – you can find yourself spending hours online without realising it – and this can be intensely annoying for people trying to get through to you. This also applies if someone wants to send you a fax. If you have a large family, hogging the telephone line for hours on end can also cause friction.

Another good reason for installing a dedicated telephone line just for internet use is that you can talk to your ISP's technical support staff on the phone *and* connect to the internet at the same time. This can be very useful if you're trying to sort out problems, because you can test their suggested remedies without having to hang up.

Hanging up can be bad for your health. Helplines often use an automated telephone queueing system

> **TIP**
>
> *If you have a second telephone line installed for internet use, make sure you tell the telephone company that this is what it is for, so they can supply you with the right sort of connection.*

that directs your call to whoever's available. So if you've spent a long time explaining your internet problem to one technician, it can be extremely frustrating having to explain it all again to another technician when you ring back. An extra line also helps you keep a tab on your internet call costs, which can mount up alarmingly, especially if you surf extensively during the day, when call costs are most expensive.

Not all lines are the same

If you do go ahead and get a second line installed purely for internet use, tell the telephone company that this is what you want it for. Otherwise, the company might just fit a device that lets two telephone lines share the same connection back to the exchange. This is called Digital Access Carrier Service (DACS). It can have the effect of halving your modem speed, leading to slower download times and a more frustrating web experience.

Making one line go further

If installing a second line is too much bother or expense, there are software packages available now that can monitor your telephone connection while you're online. For example,

Software packages such as Internet Call Manager can monitor your telephone connection while you're online.

Getting Started

Internet Call Manager (www.internetcallmanager.com), from AOL-owned InfoInterActive Corporation, tells you if someone is trying to ring you while you're online. The software gives you the option to handle such calls in a number of ways. For example, you can transfer them to your mobile phone or ask the caller to leave a voicemail. Of course, you have to pay for such services, although the software is free to download. So it's a question of weighing up how much you'd save by not installing a second line and paying the monthly line rental on it against the running costs of such a call manager.

There are other software programs that can help you make the most out of your single telephone line. Many homes these days have more than one PC, but only one may have a modem installed. You could install a second line and buy a second modem, but that would be expensive and potentially a waste of time, given that high-speed connections should soon be the norm (more on *Faster Surfing, pages 77–89*).

Now there are software solutions to help you give net access to both PCs without having to install a second line and buy a second modem. Microsoft's Internet Connection Sharing (ICS) software enables your wired-up PC to act as a gateway to the net for your other PC. Two members of your family could be online at the same time, one sending e-mail from one PC, say, the other surfing the net on the other. As they'll be sharing the same connection it does mean they may experience slower connection and download speeds, especially if both are downloading files and programs at the same time. For normal surfing though, the difference should be barely noticeable.

> **TIP**
>
> *You may find it cheaper to use a call manager software program than to install a second telephone line exclusively for internet use.*

ICS is quite tricky to configure and you have to set up both computers so that they are 'networked'. This involves making sure there is a network interface card in each PC and that they can handle *TCP/IP*. ICS is only available in Windows 98 Second Edition and later operating systems, including Windows XP. To install ICS you go to 'Control Panel', 'Add/Remove Programs', 'Windows Setup', then scroll down to 'Communications', highlight it, then click on the 'Details' tab. Check the box next to 'Internet Connection Sharing', click 'OK', then 'Apply'. After that, have your operating system installation disk at the ready and follow the on-screen prompts which take you through the installation process.

If you encounter problems, there are plenty of ICS-related articles on **Microsoft's** website (http://search.support. microsoft.com). There are also alternatives to ICS on the market, such as **WinProxy** (www.winproxy.com), Wingate (www.wingate.com) and **Sygate** (www.sygate. com).

How do I actually get connected?

Normally, when you're installing the software offered by your ISP, there will be a step-by-step on-screen guide through the connection procedure. The most important bit is telling your modem which number to dial to get through to your ISP. You also have to tell your computer what your ISP's computers are called when setting up an e-mail account (for more on e-mail *see E-mail, pages 91–112*).

Usually, your ISP will have an icon on your desktop which you click on to trigger the automatic dial-up process. If your modem is on and connected properly to the telephone socket, you should hear a faint 'peep peep peep' as the number is dialled. You then hear a combination of bizarre whooshing sounds and beeps, just like the burble a fax makes, as the computers try to talk to one another.

Depending on the ISP, you then go through an online security check of your user name and password – you usually set these up when loading the software. Such security can be quite useful to prevent people logging on to your ISP in your name and sending unflattering e-mails to your boss, for example, or, perhaps worse, reading unflattering mail sent to you.

Depending on how your ISP has configured its software, the web browser should automatically open at this point. But you don't have to do it this way. You can click on the browser icon on your desktop first, open the browser window, and then decide which of your ISPs you want to connect to (remember, there are loads of free ISPs available now, so you can run several ISPs alongside each other at no extra cost).

If you have a 'connect automatically' box ticked, the dialler will just go ahead and dial through to your default ISP. If not, you can select your chosen ISP at this point before clicking on the 'connect' button.

What if I can't connect?

Unfortunately, there are a number of things that can go wrong when trying to connect. My advice is to phone your ISP first if you encounter problems, even if you have to pay handsomely for the technical support. This is better than fiddling with settings yourself if you don't really know what you're doing. Speaking personally, I have found the 'Help' sections that come with software packages next to useless.

Your ISP should be able to take you through all the possible causes of the problem step by step. Some common reasons for a failure to connect are:

❶ No modem detected – if you have an external modem it may not be switched on or it may be plugged into the wrong socket at the back of your computer. It may also mean that the software accompanying the modem wasn't installed correctly. You may have to re-install it.

❷ No dial tone detected – it could be that the telephone cable isn't inserted into the wall socket properly, or that the socket itself is faulty. If you're using a 'splitter' connector so that you can share the socket with a telephone, the connector itself may be faulty. Check that the line is OK by inserting a telephone jack into the socket and listening for a dial tone. If you still don't hear anything, there's a fault on the line.

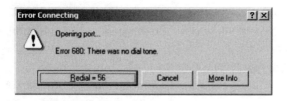

❸ Number engaged – at busy times of the day it is sometimes difficult to get through to your ISP. Good ISPs will have several numbers for you to use should you fail to get through on the main one. The simplest thing to do is leave it for a couple of minutes and then try again.

❹ Password not recognised – when installing your ISP software and going through the set-up and registration process, you normally have to enter a user name and password. This is often assigned to you and many free ISPs don't bother with this. If you've entered the password incorrectly, and then told your computer to remember the incorrect password, you'll never get through! Try retyping the password in the 'Dial-up connection' box, taking care to get it exactly right. Sometimes it's not your fault at all and there's a glitch in your ISP's security systems. Again, it's as well to check with them.

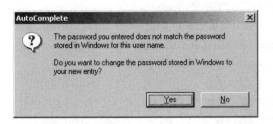

⑤ Protocol problems – sometimes your modem will have difficulty 'talking' to your ISP's modem. This could be to do with your **TCP/IP** settings – apologies for the jargon, but it's unavoidable sometimes. TCP/IP (Transport Control Protocol/Internet Protocol) is the standard way computers talk to each other on the internet. Your computer has a unique **IP address** – usually four sets of digits separated by dots – as does every other computer on the net. This helps all the information flying across the global network to arrive at the right place. Computers called Domain Name System (DNS) servers attribute names to the numbers to make the net a friendlier place. You may have to enter your ISP's exact IP address – ask your ISP for help on this one. A word of warning: sometimes when you load another ISP's software on to your system, it can interfere with the IP settings you've entered for your other ISP(s). If this happens, you'll have to re-enter them. It's a good idea to make a note of them somewhere for future reference. It will save a potentially expensive call to a helpline.

> **TIP**
>
> *Make a note of your IP settings for each ISP so that you can re-enter them if you need to.*

⑥ You connect, but it keeps disconnecting for no reason – this often happens if you have 'call waiting' on your line. The beep that you hear when you're on the phone normally interferes with the net connection and your modem drops the call. Ask your telephone company how to activate and deactivate call waiting. Another reason may be that your web browser settings are configured to drop the connection if there's a period of inactivity. The website – an online bank, for example – may do this too for your own security.

Chapter 2

Web Browsers

What is a web browser and why do I need one?

A web browser is a software program that helps you surf the net. Web pages are downloaded into the browser's window. You can type in web addresses and go to different sites, go backwards or forwards through web pages, and store your favourite website addresses in directories that you can organise in your own way. They can provide access to electronic mail, news and chat services. And the latest versions of web browsers will also help you screen websites and check them for authenticity and security.

When an internet service provider sends you a CD-ROM containing its software, most of it is actually the browser software. Although there are several web browsers to choose from, by far the most popular are:

● **Microsoft Internet Explorer** (IE) – **www.microsoft.com**
● **Netscape Navigator** (its enhanced version is called **Netscape Communicator**) – **www.netscape.com**

IE is now the dominant browser, with well over 50% of the market, having seen off its rival Netscape quite

Netscape Navigator is the main rival browser to Microsoft's Internet Explorer.

convincingly. Navigator is generally preferred by Mac users, although IE is usually pre-installed on new Macs these days. Other simpler browsers include:

- **Opera** – www.opera.com
- **Lynx** (a text-only browser) – www.lynx.browser.org
- **1X** (a stripped-down browser still capable of handling animated graphics on the net) – **www.scitrav.com**
- **Mozilla** (another simple browser designed to be compatible with all that the web can throw at it) – www.mozilla.org

You may wonder, what is the use of a browser that can't handle pictures, given the net's penchant for graphics?

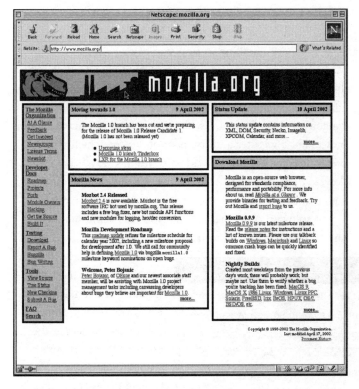

Popular alternatives to IE and Netscape include Opera (www.opera.com) and Mozilla (www.mozilla.org), pictured above.

Well, graphics take up a lot of memory and downloading them takes time. If it's information you're after, and you want it fast, a web browser that ignores graphics will be a lot quicker.

Also, the alternative browsers tend to be simpler, taking up less memory on your hard drive. In theory, this means that there is less that can go wrong. It also means that if you have a rather old computer, there is more chance that it will be able to handle the simpler browsers. It is worth asking yourself whether you really need all the functions that come with the leading browsers.

Can I have more than one browser?

Yes. There's nothing to stop you having a number of browsers on your system – you don't have to stick with the browser your ISP has given you. CD-ROMs accompanying computer and internet magazines often contain the latest versions of the various browsers available. You can load them on to your computer and try them out to see which you prefer. It is far quicker to load software this way – downloading browsers from the net can take hours, especially with a slow modem.

All software programs can develop glitches from time to time, so it's just as well to have a back-up. What you do tend to find is that each browser will try to make itself the 'default', or main, browser when you load it. When you try to connect to the net the 'default' browser program will automatically launch. But you can switch between browsers relatively easily. These days it is also possible for different browsers to read your collection of favourite websites (called 'Bookmarks' in Netscape Navigator and 'Favorites' in Microsoft Internet Explorer).

In my view there's not much difference between all the various browsers, so it's really just a question of personal preference.

> **TIP**
>
> *If you want to find information on the web and are not interested in graphics, you may find that a text-only browser suits you best. It will save you time, as it is much quicker to download words than images.*

Keeping your browser up to date

The problem with software companies is that they keep bringing out newer versions of their browsers (usually denoted by an ascending numerical series – 4.1, 4.2 etc). And as website design becomes more sophisticated, incorporating animation and sound, for example, we need the latest versions of browsers to read these pages properly.

Many people encountered problems trying to use the latest online banking and stockbroking web services because they had older versions of browsers that couldn't handle the new user name and password security features introduced by the websites. So when you've chosen your browser(s), it is very important to keep a lookout for upgrades. Regularly peruse the software company's website for upgrade news.

Another problem is that the more sophisticated web browsers become, the more sophisticated computers have to be to run them. Some of the newest versions of browsers are not compatible with older operating systems. So you have to find the browser version that is most compatible with your operating system. Your ISP should be able to give you advice. Yes, it is fiddly and annoying and all part of the general conspiracy to keep us buying new computers and new software. But the net is developing at such a pace that to make the most of what it can offer does require the latest hardware and software. That's just a fact of life online. This book assumes that you have the latest browser versions anyway.

Getting to know your browser

You should get to know your browser intimately because it's the main tool you use to surf the net. It's there to make surfing the web easier and faster for you, so the more effort you put into discovering all its functions, the more rewarding your experience will be.

The web address bar | Address ℰ http://www.sunday-times.co.uk/

This is the white bar or box usually at the top of the web browser. It's where you type in web addresses that take you to specific sites. In Internet Explorer the word 'Address:' is next to the box; in Navigator there's a little arrow. Other browsers may say 'URL' next to it. You just type the address accurately in the box, making surely you're at the start of the box, press return, and away you go. For further information on web addresses, *see page ??*.

The 'Forward' and 'Back' arrows | ⇐ Back ▾ ➡ ▾

The clever thing about browsers is that they store the pages you visit while you're online. So if you flit from website to website, it is possible to go back to one you've left, simply by clicking on the 'back' arrow button in the browser's task or menu bar. Similarly with the 'forward' arrow button.

It's exactly like flicking backwards and forwards through the pages of a book. There's no need to retype web addresses each time.

TIP

It is quite common for people to read about a website in the paper, say, write down its address, then enter that address into a search directory, such as Yahoo! or Excite. You don't have to do this! The address will take you directly to the site.

Opening new browser windows

An even quicker way to flick between different websites is to open a new window in your browser. In the latest versions of both leading browsers, you do this by clicking on the 'File' tab, selecting 'New' and then 'Window' or 'New Navigator Window'. The same web page you're on will then load into this new window. But if you type a new address into the address bar, or select a new bookmark, the new website will load into this window. The old website is still loaded in the other browser window.

You can then switch quickly between the websites by clicking on tabs at the bottom of the screen. And if you want to be really clever, you can minimise the browser screens and arrange them so that two or more browser windows are side by side, allowing you to compare and contrast websites, or absorb information from several sources at once.

The 'Stop' button

This humble button is actually very important because it stops you wasting time. When the web is busy it can almost grind to a halt, especially when downloading graphics, which take up a lot of memory. If you get fed up of waiting, just click the stop button and move on to something else. If you don't, your browser and modem will continue labouring away trying to download the pages in the background while you're trying to look at another website, slowing up the process even further.

The 'Refresh' or 'Reload' button

Sometimes web pages don't always load properly first time – some of the data gets lost on its travels, leaving an incomplete picture or piece of text. If you click on the 'Refresh' or 'Reload' button your browser will simply try to download the page again, hopefully with more luck. Another use for this button is to keep web pages up to date. Some websites, such as financial data providers, provide information that is constantly updated – share prices, for example. If you are online for a while, you should refresh the page every so often – if it doesn't do so automatically – and you'll then receive the very latest information.

Other useful functions

As Microsoft and Netscape compete with each other, they bring out newer versions of their browsers, laden with yet more features. Most of them are based on the bookmark principle, giving you short-cuts to web services such as radio stations, shopping sites and search directories. Really, there's no reason why you can't find these services yourself without having dedicated buttons built into the browser software.

So here's a round-up of the browser features you *will* find useful:

- **Home** 🏠 clicking on this button takes you back to the first page that loads when you first log on to the net. Whenever you load an ISP's software, they usually make their own website your default home page. But you can choose any website you like. Or you can choose to start with a blank page. In Internet Explorer go to 'Tools', 'Internet Options', then type in the web address of the site you would like as your home page. In Navigator you click on 'Edit', 'Preferences' and follow the same procedure.

- **The Print button** 🖨 once you've found an article or picture you like you can print it off there and then.

- **E-mail button** 📧 this enables you to launch your e-mail software from the browser (for more on e-mail, *see E-mail, pages 91–112*).

- **History** 🕑History you can see all the websites you have visited recently. This is useful if you came across a good site but forgot to bookmark it. You can specify how long you want your History folder to keep records for. If you specify '0' days, it will only show you the websites you've visited today.

- **Security** – the latest version browsers have a whole host of security features to help you filter out websites you deem unsuitable and check whether the sites you visit offer secure, encrypted transactions. *See Safety, Security and your Rights, pages 237–273*, for more on security issues.

● **Save** – as well as being able to bookmark pages so you can return to them when you're online, you can also save specific web pages to read offline. In the latest browser versions you get a choice as to the way you want to save the page. For example, you can tell your browser to save just the text, not the pictures, or the whole caboodle, animated graphics and all.

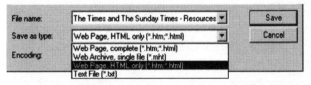

● Another way to **capture text** on a web page is to highlight it by clicking and dragging over the desired paragraphs using your mouse. Once you've highlighted the text, right click on it, choose 'Copy', open a new word processing document, then choose 'Paste' to insert the text into the new document. You can also save specific images by pointing at them, right clicking, then choosing 'Save as'.

● **Send** – if you come across a website that you'd like to tell someone else about, you can send the link or the entire page to them by choosing 'Send' from the 'File' menus of both types of browser. You then send an e-mail to the recipient, so you'll need to know their e-mail address (*see Chapter 6, pages 91–112*, for more on e-mail).

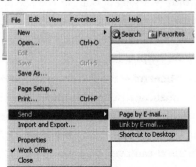

Web addresses explained

Web addresses need some explanation. A web address is a combination of words and symbols that directs you to a particular website, or particular page on a website. The **www** bit of a web address is probably the most widely recognised symbol of the net. Not many companies advertise without including their web address these days.

You may have heard people talk about **URLs** – Uniform Resource Locators. It's just net-nerd-talk for web address. If you're new to it all, the motley collection of dots, dashes, hyphens and abbreviations that makes up a web address can be off-putting. So let's take an example and break it down into its constituent parts.

The Sunday Times newspaper's web address is: http://www.sunday-times.co.uk

Each colon and forward slash is essential – just a missing dot and your browser will tell you it couldn't find the website. Some web addresses may also be case-sensitive, so be careful not to put in any capitals where they don't belong.

The **http://** bit tells you that the site is on the World Wide Web. You don't need to know this, but **http** stands for Hypertext Transfer Protocol. It's just another of these web standards agreed by programmers and designers and is not worth worrying about. All website addresses begin with **http://**. So when you see web addresses written down like this: **www.randomname.com**, it is assumed that you'll type in the **http://** bit first.

Thankfully, these days the latest versions of browsers will automatically put in the **http://** for you if you forget. They will also guess which web address you're beginning to type and try to complete it for you. If it's a particularly well-known site you can even type just the main part of the name and the browser will fill in the rest of the address for you.

Ironically, although the **www** bit is the most widely recognised symbol of the internet, not all web addresses include it. Normally the name of the company or organisation comes after the **www** or **http:**// bit, followed by an abbreviation which tells you broadly what kind of organisation it is. The most common abbreviation is **.com**, which is short for commercial and is used predominantly by US companies.

In the UK, companies commonly have **.co.uk** after their names; German websites may have **.de**, but there's nothing stopping UK or German companies having **.com** after their names either. It can get very confusing. So you shouldn't assume you know where a company or organisation is based just by its web address. The whole point about the net for many is that it is global and crosses national boundaries.

Educational institutions often include the abbreviation **.ac** for academic, and non-commercial organisations may have **.org** in their address. Government departments will usually have **.gov** in there somewhere. Another common abbreviation is **.net**.

These names and the accompanying abbreviations are called *domain names* and the system for organising and classifying them all is called the *Domain Name System* **(DNS)**. The computers that translate all these names back into Internet Protocol addresses – that unique set of identifying numbers mentioned in Chapter 1 *(see page 29)* – are called domain name servers.

It's a thorny issue as to who should control the available names and abbreviations. One thing is certain, if the number of websites keeps increasing at the same rate we will need more of them.

You can register any domain name you think of with a number of agencies. Some bright sparks registered hundreds of names that companies and organisations were likely to want. Some domain names have changed hands for millions of dollars, such is the perceived importance of having your company's brand name in your web address. But you have to be careful. Just registering names that are very similar to big brand names in the hope of making an easy buck could land you in hot water. It could be interpreted that you are passing yourself off as the company itself for possibly fraudulent reasons.

Once you've typed in the website address accurately and pressed return, you should go straight through to the website's **home page**. This is the opening page of the website that usually tells you about the company or service and what it offers. Each website can have hundreds of pages, and each of those separate pages can have a different address.

If you go through to the Sunday Times home page, it looks like this:

A typical web page will have a menu of items on the left taking you to different sections of the website.

Non 'http' addresses

The web is only one part of the internet. Two other significant parts are **FTP (File Transfer Protocol) sites**, mostly dedicated to distributing software across the net, and **Usenet**, the collective name for news discussion groups. FTP web addresses start **ftp://** and Usenet addresses begin with an abbreviation such as **alt.** or **news.** – for more on this, *see pages 136–139.*

Bookmarking websites and web pages

Each page on a website has a unique address that usually gets longer and longer the further you explore a website. If you wanted to go back to that page at a later date, one way would be to write down the exact address of that page, with all its slashes, abbreviations and so on. This isn't practical, to say the least. The likelihood of a mistake is very high and it also wastes time.

If the website has been designed using 'Frames' – a way of organising the page so that there is a fixed frame of information enclosing pages that can change within the frame – the web address will not change even if you click through to different parts of the website. This could make finding a particular page again even trickier.

Luckily, there is an easy way to store website addresses. Bookmarking is the best thing your web browser can do. Instead of having to remember ludicrously long web addresses you can just tell your browser to remember the page you're on. With Netscape Navigator, you click on the 'Bookmarks' pull-down menu and click the 'Add Bookmark' option. With Microsoft's Internet Explorer you click on the 'Favorites' pull-down menu and then click on 'Add To Favorites'. You can also click on the right mouse button while pointing at the page and you'll be offered the same options. Or you can just hold down the 'Control' button and press 'D' on your keyboard and it will bookmark the page in both browsers.

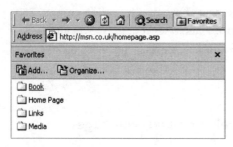

Bookmarking pages is the best thing your browser can do.

Bear in mind that when you do this you will bookmark the precise page you're on. So if you like the site as a whole, and not just the specific page you happen to be looking at, go back to the home page first before bookmarking.

Working offline

When bookmarking websites, you can also tell your browser to store all the pages on your computer's hard drive so that you can view them again without having to go online. This is a useful feature that can help cut down your telephone bill. Of course, it is best suited to sites whose information isn't likely to change very often, otherwise you may end up reading stuff that is out of date. To prevent this happening you can also tell your browser to check for updated versions of the saved pages next time you go online. You can then save the new pages for offline viewing later.

You can also ask a website called a *notifier* (such as **www.netmind.com**) to tell you when a particular web page you've bookmarked is updated. You just tell the notifier your e-mail address (*see E-mail, page 94*) and the URL of the page you want monitored.

Organising your bookmarks

Bookmarking is essential for navigating the net, especially as it becomes ever more complicated and crowded. The latest versions of web browsers also allow you to organise your bookmarks in any way you want. For example, if you're particularly keen on wine websites, you can create a folder called 'Wine' and every time you visit a wine site you like, bookmark it to this folder. Obviously, the same goes for any subject. In Internet Explorer you choose 'Organize Favorites' from the 'Favorites' menu. In Netscape you can choose 'Communicator', 'Bookmarks', 'Manage Bookmarks' or, more directly, click on the dedicated 'Bookmarks' tab and then choose 'Manage Bookmarks'.

When you tell your browser to bookmark a page, it will often give the file a very long title – whatever the site uses to introduce itself. For example, if you bookmarked a fictitious wine site called DrinkYourselfStupid.co.uk, the bookmark title might say: 'Welcome to Drink Yourself Stupid, the UK's premier wine website for bibulous buffoons'. You don't need all that, so you can shorten it to Drink Yourself Stupid or DYS if you want.

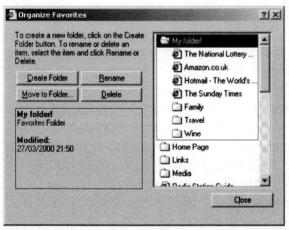

Organising your favourite bookmarks in Internet Explorer.

If you want to return to a favourite site, all you do is click on the 'Bookmarks' or 'Favorites' tab located in your browser's menu bar. A pull-down menu will list all your bookmarks. Just click on the one you want and you'll be whisked straight through to the website.

Understanding web pages

Web pages are generally written in a computing language called **HTML** – HyperText Mark-up Language. That's all you really need to know! They usually look pretty much like standard magazine pages, using pictures, text and colour. But they can be much more dynamic than conventional pages because they can also accommodate moving pictures and sound.

They use **hyperlinks** which are bits of text or images that take you somewhere else once you've clicked on them, or launch a snippet of audio or video. For example, if you're on a web page and you see a link with a little speaker icon next to it, you know that if you click on the link you'll hear a snippet of sound – whatever that may be. You need the right

```
<HEAD><TITLE>The Sunday Times </TITLE>
<!—Main frame set for Sunday Times Front page—>
<!—Day_root /sti/2000/03/26/—>
<!—Issue 9161—>
</HEAD>

<frameset BORDER="0" cols="*,640,*">
        <frame  SRC="/standing/shared/bg.n.html" MARGIN-
WIDTH="0" MARGINHEIGHT="0" FRAMEBORDER="NO">

<FRAMESET COLS="95,*" BORDER="0">
<FRAME NAME="left" SRC="/news/pages/sti/2000/03/26/lefttoday.n.html"
MARGINWIDTH="0" MARGINHEIGHT="0" FRAMEBORDER="NO"
SCROLLING="auto" NORESIZE>
<FRAME NAME="frame2"
SRC="/news/pages/sti/2000/03/26/frame2fpsti.n.html"  MARGIN-
WIDTH="0" MARGINHEIGHT="0" FRAMEBORDER="NO">
```

A sample of HTML text, the hidden coding that underlies most web pages.

software to make the most of these **multimedia** features, and this is dealt with in the next section.

Most text hyperlinks – now just called links – are easy to spot because the text is usually a different colour and underlined. But web design has moved on apace. These days links can change colour once your mouse pointer lands on them. You might see a drop-down menu appear, for example, containing other links to other parts of the website. When you're pointing at a link you will also see more information about it given in a bar at the bottom of your browser. This might be explanatory text or the web address of the site you'd go to if you clicked on the link.

Another way of knowing that you're on a link is that your mouse pointer will change shape to a pointing hand icon. This is especially useful when pointing at images that are links. When the pointer icon changes to a hand you know that if you click on the link you'll be whisked off to another web page. If the icon doesn't change, the image isn't a link.

Chapter 3

Navigating the Net

Introduction – Big and getting bigger

So now you're up and running and connected (we hope) to the net. That's the easy part. Finding your way around it and pinpointing the information or service you want is much harder. At the last count, there were over eight billion pages on the World Wide Web, with hundreds more being launched every day. As the global internet population is expected to reach one billion over the next few years, the number can only increase as more services go online to cater for the increase in demand.

Once you've got to grips with your browser you'll want to find out what's out there. After all, it's no use knowing how to type in web addresses if you don't know the address in the first place! If you're after something specific, navigating your way through this cyber equivalent of the Tower of Babel can be tricky, if not exasperating.

In this chapter we'll show you that acquainting yourself with just a few basic rules can help you get to where you want to go a lot faster. But bear in mind that part of the fun of the net is surfing pretty aimlessly just to see what's out there. You never know what you may find.

Keeping it simple

The net can be as complicated or as simple as you like. Plenty of net users exist quite happily just making the most of the sites listed on their ISP's home page. A good ISP tries to make sure that there is enough to inform and entertain its users, if only to prevent them flitting off to other sites to the annoyance of its advertisers.

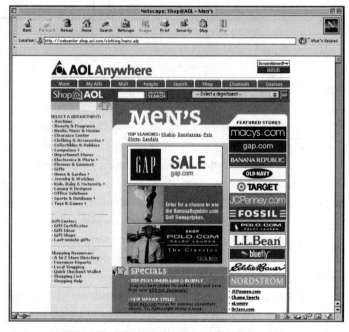

AOL (above, www.aol.com) and CompuServe (opposite, www.compuserve.com) are two of the largest proprietary ISPs.

Proprietary ISPs, such as America On-Line (AOL) and CompuServe, try even harder to keep their members within an exclusive environment. The belief is that members will be prepared to carry on paying monthly subscription fees if

they feel they are receiving services not available elsewhere on the web.

Newspapers are increasing their internet coverage by the day, with website reviews and recommendations, and internet and PC magazines also contain tons of website addresses for you to try out. The secret of successful surfing is remembering to bookmark good websites when you visit them.

Before we even get on to using search engines and directories, it's worth pointing out that you may be able to find what you want just by using your browser and guessing. For example, if you're looking for a well-known company's website, it's a good bet that its name is included in the web address. So typing **www.companyname.co.uk** into the address box and hitting 'return' may well get you to where you want to go. But this approach is risky if you want to prevent children from accessing unsuitable content.

Even if you haven't got the address exactly right, it's likely that the company will have registered all the web addresses that look similar. Your incorrect attempt could still be forwarded to the correct website. Even if you're not this lucky, a little fiddling around with alternative endings, such as **.com** or **.net**, coupled with the odd hyphen between words, will often do the trick.

Using search engines and directories

Having said all this, the first port of call for most people is a search engine or *directory*. In theory, these are websites that help you find anything that's on the net just by keying in a few search words in a search box. The truth is

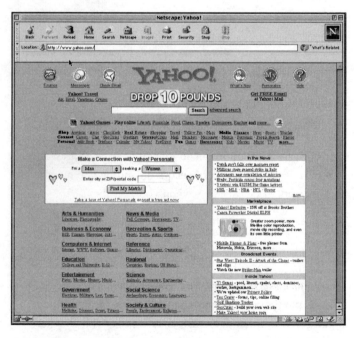

One of the earliest search engines, Yahoo! (www.yahoo.com), has now evolved into a giant portal site.

less satisfactory. There is simply so much available on the net these days – from the erudite to the downright dangerous – that finding precisely what you want has become an often frustrating and time-consuming process.

Even though search facilities have improved a great deal, I have to confess that I'm not a great fan of them in general. I'd much rather have someone tell me the web address of a specific recommended site than root around on a search engine that may or may not find what I'm looking for. **Yahoo!** (www.yahoo.com) may have started out life as a search engine, but it quickly realised that there was far more mileage in becoming an all-singing all-dancing *portal* site. It may be the biggest and most well-known portal site in the world, but some critics say it has virtually given up on the idea of trying hard to index the web.

A portal is a general-purpose website that usually contains its own entertainment and information services as well as links to many others. They tend to aggregate services so that their sites will become a destination in their own right, so they are sometimes called *aggregator* sites, too. The search engine or directory often seems like an afterthought.

One common misconception among people new to the net is that *everything* is online, as if the net has magically put the world's knowledge base online. This is far from the case. Stuff is on the net only if someone has been bothered to put it there. It still has a long way to go before it rivals the resources of a national library, for example. But it is getting there. Even the *Encylopaedia Britannica* has succumbed to the pressure and disgorged its contents on to the web.

Comprehensiveness versus ease of use

For the purists out there, a search *engine* is different to a search *directory*. An engine involves a program called a spider or robot scouring all websites it can get access to, recording all the information, and depositing it in huge

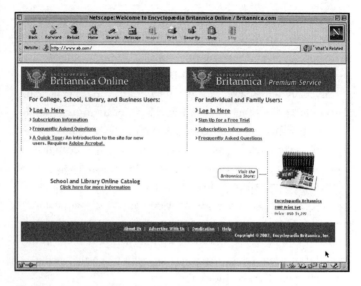

The Encyclopaedia Britannica *(www.eb.com) site.*

databases. These spiders can search as many as a thousand pages per second. When you type in a word or phrase the search engine will throw up all documents containing those words or phrases.

This is a very powerful tool, given the amount of data available on the net, especially if you are carrying out academic research and thoroughness is essential. The problem is that if you are not specific enough in your choice of words you can still end up with millions of irrelevant documents that are little help to man or beast. Sifting through them can take hours, many of them wasted. This is not made any easier by the fact that there are now an estimated eight billion web pages on the net. In 1995 there were just 100,000 websites.

Search directories take a more selective approach, with people deciding what is and isn't worth categorising for their users. Rather than carrying out blanket searches, you can narrow down the field by pre-selecting a category, such as

Sport or Shopping. This makes it much more likely that you'll find a site that is relevant and interesting. But this kind of indexation does mean that you cannot be sure you've found everything that's out there on the subject you're interested in. You'll only be shown what the search directory company has decided to record and categorise.

And there's the rub. Search directories have realised that indexing and categorising everything on the net is well nigh impossible. It comes as a shock to many to learn that even the biggest search directories cover just 20% of all websites on average. Now this isn't a problem if they correctly guess what surfers are most likely to be interested in and what sites aren't worth including at all. And let's face it, there is a lot of dross out there. But comprehensiveness is obviously sacrificed on the altar of speed and convenience.

These days, the distinction between engines and directories is becoming blurred, and you'll often hear the terms used interchangeably. In this book, for instance! Despite

> **TIP**
>
> *No search engine lists all websites, so if you look for a site and don't find it, it doesn't mean it isn't out there. Try using a different search engine!*

the rise of UK-specific directories, there is still a bias towards US-based websites, which can be frustrating. And many websites complain that, even though they register with the leading directories, it is a lottery as to whether their company will come up in a relevant search.

The trend is towards more and more specialist directories – a natural and welcome response to the burgeoning size of the web. For example, **Seniors Search** (www.seniorssearch.com) is a directory dedicated to collating sites that may be of interest to the over-fifties. **ShopSmart** (http://uk.shopsmart.com) lists and reviews online retailers and compares prices. The **Internet Movie**

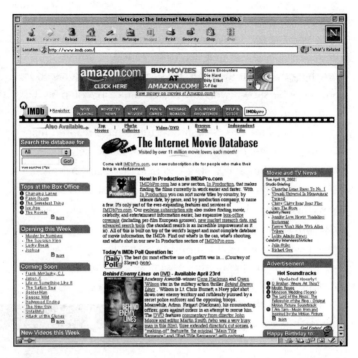

If movies are one of your great interests, then check out the Internet Movie Database (http://www.imdb.com) search directory.

Database (http://www.imdb.com) does what its name suggests and a lot more besides.

Increasingly, search engines such as **AltaVista** (http://uk.altavista.com) allow you to search for just image, video or audio files, as well as standard web pages. You can often specify the time-frame for your search, to weed out old documents or articles that aren't relevant any more.

There are also a number of so-called ***meta-search engines*** that search a number of directories simultaneously. This is a very useful development given that one engine's database can differ markedly from another's. Most engines can also rank the results of your search according to their relevance and the number of search words found.

Search engines can also be used for finding public e-mail addresses, and there are plenty of electronic equivalents of the local business directory to help you find useful services – **Yellow Pages** (www.yell.com), for example. There are also services, such as price comparison agents, that will scour the net for you looking for bargains.

But in short, there is still a long way to go before directories are sophisticated enough to be able to pinpoint surfers' requests speedily and accurately whilst remaining straightforward to use.

So what are the best search engines to use?

A lot depends on what you're looking for. If you're doing intense academic research, then you need a really comprehensive engine or specialist directory relevant to the work you're doing. An engine like **Copernic** (www.copernic.com) will trawl through at least 13 other search engines, directories, Usenet lists and e-mail databases looking for what you want. You need to download its browser software, which is closely integrated into Internet Explorer, but once you've done this you have an excellent search tool on your desktop capable of saving and categorising your searches. Of course, searching such a large number of other engines does take longer, but it's generally worth it.

For very specific lists of sites grouped according to minority-interest categories, you could try **Webdata** (www.webdata.com), or **GoGettem** (www.gogettem.com). If you're just looking for good online shops to buy CDs from, you should be OK with the big name engines and directories (*see pages* 60–61). Much of the time it's a case of trial and error – which is why I don't like them very much!

There is a site called **Search Engine Watch** (www.searchenginewatch.com) that looks at all the latest developments in search engines, gives opinions on which are

Two popular search engines, AltaVista (top, www.altavista.com) and
Copernic (bottom, www.copernic.com).

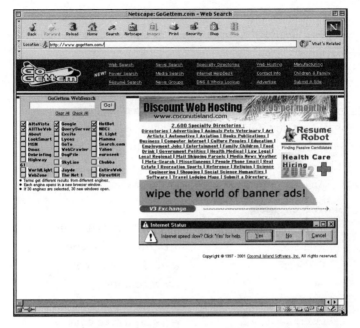

Gogettem is one of several meta-search engines. These expand your search by using lots of other search engines as well.

the best, and provides more tips on how to conduct accurate searches. Don't forget to bookmark your favourite search engines for ease of access. You could set up a dedicated 'Search' folder within your browser in which to keep them all. Browsers also have 'Search' tabs on their menu bars that take you to various search engines.

One search engine that has been winning plaudits for its speed and accuracy is **Google** (www.google.com). It does not have any distracting content of its own, just a plain vanilla search box. This helps increase the search speed, which usually comes in at under 0.5 seconds. To give you some idea of the computing power involved, Google uses a mathematical equation involving over 400 million unknown variables capable of ranking all the pages listed and three billion terms. Now that's not something you can do with a pen and paper. Google has indexed over two billion web pages – impressive, but still only 25% of what's thought to be out there.

The really clever bit is that instead of searching absolutely every bit of text on a web page – a great deal of which is not relevant to your search – Google differentiates between important and unimportant sections, as indicated by the font size used, for example. It has learned to look at web pages with a discerning eye.

Anyway, here's a list of the main contenders …

Search engines

AltaVista UK	http://uk.altavista.com
Excite	http://my.excite.com
FastSearch	www.alltheweb.com
Go	www.go.com
Google	www.google.co.uk
Overture	www.overture.com
HotBot	http://hotbot.lycos.com
Lycos	www.lycos.co.uk
Mirago	www.mirago.co.uk
Northern Light	www.northernlight.com
WebCrawler	www.webcrawler.com
NBCi	www.nbci.com

Search directories

Britannica	www.britannica.com
Yahoo!	www.yahoo.com
Yahoo! UK	http://uk.yahoo.com
About.com	www.about.com
DMOZ Open Directory Project	http://dmoz.org
The Argus Clearinghouse	www.clearinghouse.net
Galaxy	www.galaxy.com
LookSmart	www.looksmart.com
Search Gate	www.searchgate.co.uk

UKdirectory	www.ukdirectory.co.uk
UKOnline	www.ukonline.com
UK Plus	www.ukplus.co.uk

Meta-search engines

All4one	www.all4one.com
Copernic	www.copernic.com
MetaCrawler	www.metacrawler.com
Dogpile	www.dogpile.com
ProFusion	www.profusion.com
Ask Jeeves	www.ask.co.uk
Powersearch	www.powersearch.com
GoGettem	www.gogettem.com

Business and phone directories

Yellow Pages	www.yell.com
Scoot	www.scoot.co.uk
BT PhoneNet UK (directory enquiries)	www.bt.com

Tracing e-mail addresses

Yahoo! PeopleSearch	http://people.yahoo.com
Bigfoot	www.bigfoot.com
WhoWhere	www.whowhere.lycos.com
Internet Address Finder	www.iaf.net

Search rules and tips

Much of the frustration associated with the use of search engines is caused by a lack of understanding about how to search. This isn't surprising as the rules are often very complicated and differ from site to site. But if you do intend to use the net a lot – and believe me, it can become addictive – taking the trouble to learn a few basic search skills pays dividends in the long run.

Logic underpins most search engines. Words such as AND, OR and NOT, whether spelled out or assumed, help computers sift vast amounts of data. These words are called **_Boolean operators_** after British mathematician George Boole.

For example, if you typed in 'dog AND bone' the search engine would find all documents where both those words were mentioned. If you wrote 'dog OR bone', the search engine would find all documents containing at least one of the words or both. This would result in a much larger, and probably unmanageable, number of documents. Searching on 'dog NOT bone' would have thrown up documents containing the word dog but not the word bone. That's Boolean logic. Other useful words include NEAR, which ensures that the words you've chosen are in close proximity and not scattered at opposite ends of a document with no relevance to each other at all.

Brackets round search words like this: (search phrase) can also tell the engine that you want to search for the phrase within the brackets exactly as written, rather than each of the component words. Again, each engine will have its own version of this, so read up on the rules. In quite a few engines speech marks – "search phrase" – will do the same thing.

These days, many search engines use their own versions of Boolean searching, assuming you want all your search words to be found, rather than just any; other search engines assume you want any of the words. To confuse things further, some search engines use Boolean logic but denoted by different symbols. For example, + and – before words can equate to AND and NOT. The treatment of upper and lower case can also be quirky.

It really is worth the effort finding out in detail the search system that a search engine or directory uses by investigating the 'Search Tips' section, usually found near the search box, or by choosing the 'Advanced Search' option. It may be uninspiring to have to do this, but it will save you time in the long run. There are search engines, such as AskJeeves, that attempt to answer questions you type into the search box. Although this is a laudable attempt to make search engines more intuitive to use, the answers you get are often completely unrelated to your question. This can even be more frustrating because the 'human' touch raises expectations of a more human response.

Berkeley, the famous US university, has a useful table on its site comparing the search features of some of the engines it recommends to its students. It is a very useful resource. Point your browser at this unwieldy address:

http://www.lib.berkeley.edu/TeachingLib/Guides/Internet/ToolsTables.html

For an excellent overview of the various search engines have a look at Berkeley University's website.

Still can't find what you're looking for?

The web is changing all the time and developing at a remarkable rate. Websites come and go and links in directories can become defunct. You'll often receive error messages telling you that the browser couldn't find the website, or the specific page you were after within a website. There can be a number of reasons for receiving error messages:

❶ **The website doesn't exist any more** – there's not much you can do about this. Sometimes you do get through to the website only to be told that it no longer exists, which is at least a little more helpful. If you're lucky you may be given a new link to go to. Directories worth their salt keep their databases up-to-date – there's nothing more annoying than a whole page of out-of-date links.

❷ **The page has been removed or updated** – the information you're after may have been moved to another part of the site. On the error message page you'll often be given the main home page web address of the site that hosted the original page. If you click on this link you can at least scour the site for the information you were after. Alternatively, you can delete part of the web address in the address box of your browser until you reach the main domain name e.g. **www.sunday-times.co.uk** and then hit return. This will take you to the website's home page, too.

❸ **You typed the address incorrectly** – you may have forgotten the dot between the www and the domain name, or misspelled the website's name. Have a look and try again.

❹ **The search directory has indexed the site wrongly** – this should be a rare occurrence. You can test it by altering the web address slightly in a number of permutations. If you eventually get through and the directory is at fault, you should let them know in the strongest possible terms!

T I P S

Here are some general tips to make searching less of a headache:

- *Try to use unique words and phrases*

- *Make sure you spell the words correctly*

- *Use several words rather than just a couple to help narrow the field down*

- *Learn how the search engine handles upper and lower case*

- *Use Boolean operators where relevant (or the search engine's own version)*

- *Compare results from several search engines or use a meta-search engine*

- *Try other sources of information within search engines, such as Usenet newsgroups, as well as the web*

- *When you're browsing all the 'hits' thrown up by a search, open new browser windows when clicking on the ones you're most interested in rather than reading each entry one by one and then pressing the back button to the results page. You'll save a lot of time this way.*

Chapter 4

Downloading Software and Files

Plug-ins

Surfing the web is now a rich multimedia experience incorporating sound, images, video and animation. To make the most of all that the web can offer you, you need the right software that will let you listen to music, for example, or watch videos. These software programs are called *plug-ins*.

Software companies are competing madly with each other to make their versions of these plug-ins the definitive version. There are no standards, so that if a video file, say, is in a format devised by one particular software company, you have to download the plug-in that can read those files. Video files in another format will require another plug-in. There are usually several programs available that do much the same thing. This can be confusing, but at least it gives you the opportunity to try out a few and see which one you like best.

The latest browsers have several essential plug-ins already built in, but you don't have to stick with these. You can download alternative programs from the software companies' websites. (Again, you can find a number of these plug-ins on

RealPlayer (above, www.real.com) is one of the leading plug-ins for music and video. Apple's version is QuickTime (below, www.apple.com/quicktime).

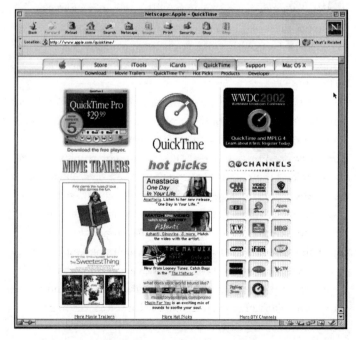

CD-ROMS that come with computer and net magazines.)
A popular program for music and video, and the one that
seems to be dominating the market, is **RealPlayer**
(**www.real.com**), which includes **RealAudio** and **RealVideo**.
Microsoft has its own version called **Windows Media Player**
incorporated into Internet Explorer. Apple's version is called
QuickTime (**www.apple.com/quicktime**).

Such plug-ins are helping to transform the music industry.
You can now listen to samples of songs online – the net's
version of the traditional listening room – to help you decide
whether you want to buy the CD. And you can even
download entire CDs on to your hard drive. For more on
downloading digital music, *see Miscellaneous Services, page
213*.

Another important program is **Shockwave Director** and
Flash (**www.shockwave.com**), which enables your browser
to handle animated graphics and other advanced website
design features. Many websites are using this program these
days, so if you don't have it, your browser won't be able to
load the page properly. Usually, if this happens, the website
provides a link to the software company so that you can
download the required software there and then. But be
warned: some of these programs are several megabytes in
size and can take a long time to download, especially with a
slow modem (28.8kbps) and at a busy time of the day.

A lot of documents on the internet are now designed
using **Adobe Acrobat** (**www.adobe.com**), which helps make
pages look exactly as they would in a conventional book or
magazine. But you need the **Acrobat Reader** plug-in to read
these files (called *PDF files*). It is well worth getting,
especially if you plan to print off documents – the quality is
excellent. Also, websites often have forms that you need to
fill in. Rather than completing them online, you can print
them off before posting.

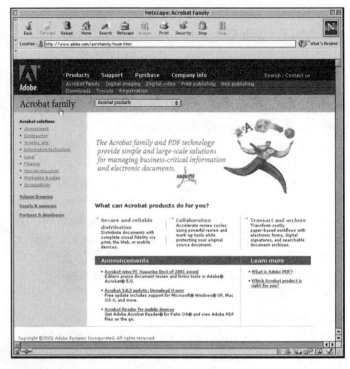

Adobe's Acrobat Reader is one of the most useful plug-ins you can have.

ActiveX controls

Other types of helper programs are called ActiveX controls, which start working as soon as they are downloaded. With most plug-ins you have to save them to a disk first, install them, then restart your computer. ActiveX controls are nimbler and have more scope. If you come across a website that requires an ActiveX control for you to read it properly, it will check your hard drive to see whether you already have it installed. If not, it will load itself on to your computer with your approval.

As ActiveX is a Microsoft invention, it is designed for use with the Internet Explorer browser. If you use a Windows 95/98/NT-compatible version of Netscape, you can configure the browser to accept ActiveX controls by downloading a plug-in called **ScriptActive**.

Java applets

Java is a programming language designed by software company Sun Microsystems to work on any computer regardless of the operating system (e.g. Windows or Mac OS). Websites can sometimes use mini-programs called *applets* which load on to your computer as and when they are needed. For example, if you launch some online services you'll see 'Loading applet...' in the status bar at the bottom of the page. The applet doesn't remain on your hard drive when you go offline, so it doesn't use up disk space.

Some websites are also designed using an addition to HTML called JavaScript, which facilitates animated graphics amongst other things. The main problem with JavaScript is that older browser versions have trouble reading it – pages often don't load properly. You can either ignore websites designed using JavaScript, or better, upgrade your browser.

Free software

The net thrives in a culture of shared knowledge and experience. Consequently, there are hundreds of sites that offer software that you can download for free.

> **TIP**
>
> *Download software early in the morning (when most Americans are still in bed), or look out for free CD-ROMS accompanying internet and PC magazines. These often have lots of useful plug-ins on them and it takes a fraction of the time loading them on to your hard drive.*

These may be enhancements to existing programs, or full programs in their own right. *Freeware* is, as its name suggests, entirely free. *Shareware* is usually free for an evaluation period, giving you the chance to try out the product before committing yourself. At the end of the evaluation period you're expected to cough up a registration fee.

It is common for shareware programs to have only a few out of many possible features activated. You can get a feel for the product and then decide either to stick with the limited free version or pay to receive the full version. So when you see lots of 'free' software advertised on computer magazine CD-ROMS, bear this in mind.

Another common practice is for software companies to release pilot versions of their products, known as **beta programs**. But be warned: these are not the finished article and often contain glitches that can interfere with other programs on your system. Net users are used as guinea pigs in effect.

The advantage is that you get to use the very latest products that could enhance your online experience greatly. If you do come across recurring errors, tell the software company and ask if there's a way to put it right. This is why they release such programs for free – to get feedback from net users and put things right before they sell them commercially.

Often, correcting errors is a simple case of downloading a line of code. An enhancement or addition to an existing program is called a **fix** or **patch**. Not many software programs are entirely glitch-free, and all can be improved. So again, it's up to you to scour software company websites on a regular basis for news of improvements to your existing programs. It's a bit like fine-tuning your car to keep it in tip-top condition.

Most programs you download will have a **.exe** extension. When you click on the file in the directory you downloaded it to, the program will unravel itself automatically. But some files you download may be in other formats. A common one is **Zip** which has a **.zip** extension. These are compressed files that don't take as long to download. To unpack these compressed files you'll need an expander program, such as **WinZip**, **ZipMagic**, **CuteZip**, or **Zip Explorer Pro**.

Some useful and popular software sites include:

Download.com   **www.download.com**

Shareware.com   **www.shareware.com**

Tucows   **www.tucows.com**

Stroud's   **http://cws.internet.com**

Tips on downloading

The first thing to say about downloading software is that it can take a very long time if the program is several megabytes in size and you only have a 56kbps modem. Deciding to download the latest version of your favourite web browser in the middle of the afternoon – usually the busiest and slowest time on the web – is not the best strategy. It is also the most expensive time to do it, even though you're usually only paying for a local rate call.

If cost is the main consideration it makes sense to wait until the evening before you start downloading, when phone rates are lower. If speed of download is your main concern, try to do it very early in the morning, when most Americans are asleep. If you're downloading from a UK site, you should find downloads happen a little quicker after midnight, when most of us are in bed.

> **TIP**
>
> *When you decide to download a program or file, you're given a choice of whether to 'save it to disk' or 'run it from its current location'. It's better to save it to your hard drive – you choose which folder you want it to go in. Some browser versions will automatically place such files in a 'Download' folder.*

You often get a better distribution speed from a dedicated FTP site, which does nothing but supply software. Servers that allow you to access them and transfer FTP files are known as anonymous FTP servers. Generally, you log in first, then browse directories and subdirectories full of files, clicking on those you want to download. These files can often have very intimidating titles consisting of a seemingly random jumble of letters and numbers, so it's very important to get the title of the file exactly right.

You'll often find that ISP or PC helpline technicians will recommend that you download a specific patch or fix to iron out glitches that occur from time to time with your system. These little programs and extra bits of code are the most likely to have uninspiring names. Be sure to write down the exact filename on a piece of paper before you go looking for it. Downloading the wrong file could have unhappy consequences for your PC, especially if it's an update for the operating system, for example.

Bear in mind that when you are downloading software you don't have to sit there watching the progress box, you can send e-mail and surf at the same time. Get into the habit of opening new browser windows. And before you go mad downloading every bit of available software on the net, consider the effect on your hard drive memory. If you have a fairly old computer, space can be used up remarkably quickly.

FTP clients

There's nothing more annoying than for your connection to break down when you're most of the way through a big, time-consuming download. You may also have to dash out, either leaving your PC online (expensive) or aborting the download altogether (maddening). More often than not you have to start all over again.

But there are special FTP programs or **clients** that help to manage your software downloads. They can stop a download half way through and begin again at a later time at the place where they left off. They can also scour the web for the best and quickest FTP sites, allow you to schedule times when you want to download and dial your modem when you're not there. When downloads are completed they can even shut down your computer for you. Some advanced versions

Programs that help you manage your software downloads can save time and remove frustration.

can chop up a program into parts and download those parts from separate servers to speed up the process. The only snag is that not all FTP servers allow downloads to be resumed part of the way through. Still, if you plan to download a lot of software an FTP program is a good idea. And many of them are free. Here are some suggestions:

GetRight	**www.getright.com**
CuteFTP	**www.cuteftp.com**
Go!Zilla	**www.gozilla.com**
NetVampire	**www.netvampire.com**
Fetch (for Macs)	**http://fetchsoftworks.com**

Faster Surfing

Introduction – the need for speed

Not for nothing has the web been dubbed the World Wide Wait. Broadly speaking, as it is a network of networks it is only as fast as the slowest link in the chain. You could have the fastest modem and computer, but if there's a bottleneck anywhere along the line, you'll find yourself tapping your fingers on the desk in frustration.

Something strange happens when we go online. We become very impatient. The net's unquestioned ability to get us information faster than ever before has raised our expectations, perhaps to unreasonable levels. What was considered a near miracle just a few years ago is pretty much taken for granted now. A great deal of hype and misunderstanding about the net has led us to expect that we can get whatever we want whenever we want it. Technology has been struggling to keep up with our galloping expectations.

So-called early adopters – the net nerds and gizmo gurus who live for every new technological development – were more tolerant of the net's failings because they knew the extraordinary amount of computing genius that lay behind this communications phenomenon. The new wave of surfers, on the other hand, who don't really care how it works – and why should they? – want it all and they want it now! In survey after survey, lack of download speed is cited as one of the major frustrations of using the net.

The problem is that as the web experience has become immeasurably richer with the addition of colour images, animation, streaming audio and video, all these extras have placed an even greater burden on the network. Image and sound files are generally much larger than simple text files. But there's only so much data you can fit down a pipe at any one time, although there are technologies around that seek to increase this by various means. Add to this increased volume of data the sheer number of new people coming online and it's no wonder the net seems to be creaking at the seams sometimes.

As fast as the technology companies that supply the net's infrastructure upgrade and improve their systems, more seems to be required of them. And the internet motorways, or **backbones**, may be the fastest fibre optic cables around, but if you've got a slow modem, vast hordes of data will come charging to your computer, only to be forced to enter in single file. Most new computers now come with a 56kbps (56 megabits per second) internal modem as standard. That's a darn sight better than 28.8kbps, but it's still nowhere near what we need to fulfil the net's potential.

Sufficient **bandwidth** is the net industry's Holy Grail – the greater the bandwidth, the more data you can fit down the pipe. At the moment, live video pictures are still rather jerky because they require so much data to be transferred at once: most computers with standard connections simply can't cope.

Luckily there are some new technologies being rolled out that should transform our collective web experience. They are so-called **broadband services** that can transfer data at up to a hundred times faster than the fastest modem. This level of service seems to have been tantalisingly close for ages. But it looks like we may finally enjoy the benefits of high-speed connections soon.

DSL – Digital Subscriber Line

There are several DSL technologies around but they all involve sending digital data down conventional telephone wires at high speed. The most common form, and the one we are being sold by British Telecom and most internet service providers – is Asynchronous Digital Subscriber Line or **ADSL**. BT calls its own branded version **BTOpenworld** (www.btopenworld.com)

This technology allows data to be transferred across the copper-wire local telephone network at up to 2Mbps (two megabits per second), 35 times faster than the fastest 56kbps modem. The asynchronous bit refers to the fact that downloading is faster than **uploading**. As most net activity involves downloading rather than uploading, this doesn't matter much.

In practice, the general public is being sold a slower service of up to 512 kilobits per second, but still nearly ten times faster than what we have at the moment. Some industry analysts believe BT is restricting the speed for ordinary customers because it doesn't want its business customers – who can pay around £30,000 a month for a 2Mbps permanent connection called a **leased line** – to migrate in droves to this cheaper service if a similar speed is on offer. BT has certainly attracted criticism for the slow roll-out of its ADSL service – which used to cost around £25 a month plus a £150 installation charge – and for its tardiness in opening up its exchanges to competition, despite regulatory warnings.

But in February 2002, after pressure from government, the regulator Oftel, and the industry, BT reduced its wholesale broadband prices to just £14.75 a month. This will allow ISPs to lower the cost of ADSL considerably.

ADSL offers many advantages. For a start, the line is always open and it's unmetered – you don't pay by the minute. This gets rid of all that logging on and off business and stops you worrying about the length of the call while you surf. It also means you can download software and memory-munching pictures and sound far more quickly, taking a lot of the waiting out of the web experience. When people send you e-mail you'll know about it instantly.

A faster, more efficient service will undoubtedly encourage more people to surf the net and for longer periods, and this will boost e-commerce.

Cable modems

The UK cable companies have been just as slow off the mark in introducing high-speed connections to the domestic market. Cable modems don't use the traditional telephone network but send data directly down fibre optic cables. At least Telewest (**www.telewest.co.uk**) has successfully launched its Blueyonder broadband service, costing between £25 and £37.50 for installation and between £25 and £33 a month rental, depending on whether you go for digital TV services as well.

NTL, the UK's largest cable operator, is also slowly rolling out its Broadband Internet service in its franchise areas, offering download speeds of up to 512kbps and upload speeds of up to 128kbps. But the company is so crippled by

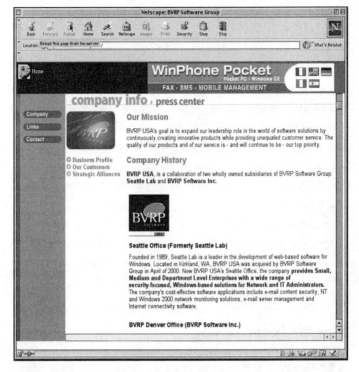

The Modem Help site (www.modemhelp.com) has excellent advice for squeezing the most speed out of your modem.

debt that customers eagerly awaiting the imminent arrival of broadband in their areas are likely to be frustrated for some time to come.

At the time of writing, NTL's service cost £24.99 a month for the 512kbps service and £14.99 for a slower 128kbps service. As the system doesn't use the voice network there are no telephone calls to pay for and your connection is permanently switched on, giving you 24-hour unmetered access to the net. You can use the telephone at the same time.

Nobody said high-speed access was going to be cheap, but at least it is getting cheaper.

ISDN – Integrated Services Digital Network

BT's forerunner to ADSL is ISDN, another higher-speed net connection enabling customers to reach speeds of up to 128kbps. It was mainly designed for the business market, but BT packaged it for the home market as Home Highway. It dispenses with the need for modems but does involve the installation of a terminal adaptor at both ends of the line. You get one normal phone connection and two ISDN connections. To get the maximum 128kbps speed you have to combine the two ISDN lines.

Again, at around £25 a month plus installation costs from £74.99, the service isn't cheap. And with the introduction of the much faster ADSL, it's no wonder that ISDN hasn't taken off in a big way in the domestic market.

Tips for faster surfing

While you contemplate which high-speed service to start saving up for, you can at least tune your PC so that it can make the most of what it's got. Here are some tips for achieving faster surfing:

❶ Always buy the fastest modem you can find (56kbps) – you'll more than recoup the cost (around £50) as faster downloads cut down your time online.

❷ Squeeze the most speed out of your modem by following the advice at the excellent **Modem Help** website (**www.modemhelp.com**).

❸ Use a Net accelerator program that can reconfigure your operating system to download data in the most efficient way and allow you to browse pages offline.

Some suggested programs:

Accelerate 2000   **www.webroot.com**
Morpheus Internet Accelerator
    www.morpheus-download-morpheus.com
SpeedNet   **www.paramagnus.com**
EasyMTU
    http://members.tripod.com/~EasyMTU/easymtu/
Tweakmaster   **www.tweakmaster.com**

❹ Learn how to use search engines effectively: it can save you a lot of time.

❺ Use the right mouse button to speed up your web browsing. Right-clicking on web pages and links calls up a neat time-saving context-sensitive menu.

❻ Take the time to customise your browser's start-up page so all the services and links you want are there ready for you when you log on.

❼ Use a diagnostic tool such as MegaPing from **Magneto Software** (**www.magnetosoft.com**) to spot log-jams at various points on the network. It could be your modem slowing things up, in which case upgrade. It may be your ISP being inefficient – consider switching to another.

❽ Make sure the serial port setting is at the right speed. For a 56kbps modem the speed should be set to 115,200bps. In Microsoft Windows, go to 'My Computer', 'Control Panel', 'Modems', 'Properties' or for Macs, go to the 'MacPPP' control panel.

❾ If you're experiencing slow connection times, ask your telephone company if the gain on the line is at the optimum level for data transfer.

⑩ Get into the habit of reading and composing your e-mail offline. It's surprising how easy it is to forget you're still online. You can tell your e-mail program to disconnect once it's downloaded all the messages.

⑪ Do your surfing at quiet times of the day. If you're looking at US sites in particular, get online in the morning when most Americans are asleep. Things can get busy and slow in the afternoons and evenings.

⑫ If it's just text-based information you're after, choose a 'text only' option if one is offered as the page will download much quicker without the graphics.

⑬ Tell your browser not to bother loading images, sound and video. Go to 'Tools', 'Internet Options', 'Advanced' in the latest version of Internet Explorer, and 'Edit', 'Preferences', 'Advanced' in Netscape Navigator.

⑭ Check the website of your modem manufacturer for any news of upgrades for the software used to run the modem (known as firmware) and also the drivers that tell your PC how to communicate with the modem.

⑮ I've said this elsewhere but it's worth saying again: don't keep clicking backwards and forwards between pages, just open new browser windows so that you can view several pages at once. It saves a lot of time.

⑯ Close other programs that you don't need open when you're surfing. This will free up more of your computer's RAM to concentrate on downloading. Ideally you should have 128MB RAM these days. Highly specified computers will have 256MB or more.

⑰ Consider using a simpler browser, such as Opera, which doesn't take up as much memory as the other popular browsers. This also helps speed things up.

Cacheing web pages

When you browse the web, your computer stores the pages you visit in a special folder on your hard drive known as your **cache** or temporary internet files. When you call up a web page in your browser which you have visited before, your computer simply takes it from its own cache file rather than wasting time downloading it from the web. This means you can also browse through these files when you're offline.

One way to speed up your browsing is to increase the amount of disk space allocated to your cache folder. Be careful though, the web page may have been updated since you last visited it, so you need to press 'Reload' or

> **TIP**
>
> *If you're accessing a page that is regularly updated (with news or financial data, for example), remember that you may be viewing an old page cached on your computer. Update the page using the* **Reload** *or* **Refresh** *button.*

'Refresh' in your browser to update the page (if your browser isn't configured to do this automatically). This is especially important when visiting financial data sites where information can change every few minutes. If you allocate too much memory to the folder, it can become unwieldy and slow your whole system down – the opposite of what you're trying to achieve. The right size cache depends on the amount of RAM you have and hard disk space. Ask your ISP for advice on the best settings for your computer.

Internet Service Providers often store copies of commonly accessed web pages on specially-assigned servers called **web proxy caches**. These can save time by intercepting your request before it has even reached the ISP's server. This means that rather than going directly to a website that could be stored halfway round the world, your request might just stay relatively local. The shorter the distance, the faster the speed of response.

Check whether your ISP uses a web proxy cache and ask how to set up your computer to make the best use of it. To bypass a cached page and go direct to the website, simply press the shift button on your keyboard and click 'Reload' or 'Refresh'.

Keeping the telephone bill down

The 'faster surfing' tips above will make your online experience more enjoyable, but they can also help keep your telephone bills down. The theory is that the faster you surf and find what you want, the less time you'll spend online. That's all very well if you are after something specific, like a sports report or bank balance. But if you're online just for entertainment – listening to the latest CD samples at an online record store, say – your concept of time can become a little blurred. Surfing should carry a health warning: it can become addictive. And with the free ISP revolution it can be tempting to think everything is for free. Until the phone bill arrives.

There are programs around that can help you monitor how long you've been online and how much it is likely to cost you. These are especially useful if other members of your family regularly surf the net and you want to keep a tight rein on the time spent online.

Try these out:

NetMeter **http://www.cracker.u-net.com/netmeter/netmeter.html**

Online Monitor **www.webutils.com/om**

WatchDog **www.sarna.net/watchdog**

The other thing you can do is shop around for a new telephone company. At last there does seem to be some real competition entering the market as the cable companies

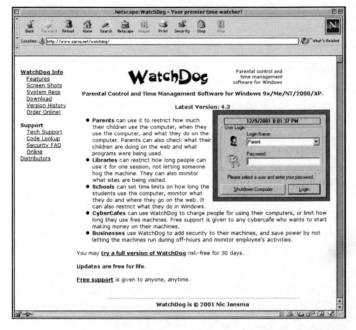

There are some very useful programs around that can help you monitor the time you've spent online, including NetMeter (www.cracker.u-net.com/netmeter/netmeter.html), WatchDog (www.sarna.net/watchdog) and Online Monitor (www.webutils.com/om).

consolidate and take on British Telecom head on. It's quite complicated working out all the different tariffs, and the best option for you will largely depend on when during the day you do most of your surfing.

For help on working out what tariff would suit you best, try useful services such as **My Call Savings** (**www.mycallsavings.com**) and **Call for Less** (**www.callforless.co.uk**). They provide tariff calculators for terrestrial phone services and mobile phones.

Some cable companies offer free local calls in the evening and at weekends – ideal for light recreational surfers. And bear in mind that you don't have to subscribe to cable to benefit from alternatives to British Telecom. For example, you can use NTL telephone services via a BT line for a £10 registration fee. This involves having an adaptor fitted to your telephone socket. You can also simply ring a three-digit code before dialing the main number to transfer you to the NTL tariff.

Another way to keep your own costs down is to surf while at work. It is very common although some companies are very strict about the amount of time you're allowed to spend online and the type of files you download. Several employees have been sacked for viewing pornography and other unsuitable sites while at work. Companies that have their own internal computer networks will guard them from outside infiltration using security systems called *firewalls*. These will often filter the type of web pages that can be downloaded, especially those that require you to enter a user name and password for security. This means that you may not be able to access some services, such as banking or stockbroking sites, from work.

If you have a tolerant employer that doesn't mind employees spending some time online for private use, you could have a chat with the information technology manager to see if there's a way you can access your sites without the company's firewall rejecting them.

Unmetered calls

With unmetered access deals you pay a fixed monthly fee rather than paying by the minute for net access. For those surfers who use the internet extensively and who have no choice but to surf during the day when calls are at their most expensive, unmetered tariffs are a godsend and should save them a considerable amount of money.

BT Openworld's Anytime service offers unlimited internet access for £14.99 per month. The cable companies NTL and Telewest, and ISPs such as Freeserve and Virgin Net, have followed suit with a range of packaged offerings.

It's less clear where the savings lie for lighter users. There is a range of tariffs, some restricting users to unlimited access just at the weekends, for example. There's no doubt that this move is a step in the right direction.

Don't confuse unmetered calls with a high-speed 'always-on' net access. Unmetered dial-up access doesn't make your connection speeds any faster. That's up to the alternative technologies mentioned above. It just so happens that ADSL and cable modems are also unmetered. Soon the only cost we'll need to worry about is the monthly all-in charge for whatever way we decide to access the net.

E-mail

What is e-mail?

Electronic mail, or e-mail, is a way of sending typed messages, documents and any other kind of digital files to other people with an internet connection and an e-mail account. When you sign up with an internet service provider, you are automatically given an e-mail address along the lines of 'yourname@ISPname.net'. You can often have several e-mail addresses. This is useful if several members of your family use e-mail – it helps messages to go to the people they were intended for.

What's so good about it?

It is easy to forget, with all the emphasis on wacky websites with fancy graphics and daft content in the media, that e-mail is the net's most successful application. The net is all about communication, after all. This relatively simple activity has revolutionised communications across the world.

The beauty and significance of e-mail is not so much the ability to communicate instantly with people across the world

– the telephone can do this after all – it's the versatility that comes with it. Along with your simple message you can attach digital files that could be whole books, pictures, sound files, or video snippets, and send them globally in a matter of seconds. And now you can send e-mails written in HTML, enabling you to incorporate graphics and links into the message itself.

Yet you can do all this at the cost of a local call, because you're still just paying for the link to your ISP. In the US, where they mostly get local calls for free, it costs them nothing. So you can send photos of the kids to relatives in far-flung parts of the world very cheaply and quickly. And when you send an e-mail to the other side of the globe, you don't have to worry about waking people up, unlike the telephone. They can just pick up the message in the morning when you've gone to bed!

Another significant advantage of e-mail is that you can send and receive messages wherever you happen to be, but the people you're communicating with don't have to know where you are. You can remain elusive yet stay in contact. It puts you in control. The reason for this is that when someone sends you an e-mail it doesn't go straight to your computer, it goes to your ISP's computers first. The messages stay there in a file reserved for your messages only. When you want to retrieve them, you go online, fire up your e-mail software and download them from your ISP's server to your computer or whichever computer you happen to be using. So you can still access your e-mail from a computer in Singapore if you like.

E-mail has also been very significant for businesses whose postal costs are often astronomical. Now they can send the same document to hundreds of recipients very easily using electronic mailing lists. There's no need to print out the document hundreds of times, put the copies in envelopes, attach stamps and find a postbox. It's all done swiftly and efficiently, saving paper, postage, storage and time.

The speed of delivery also makes it a much more efficient way of keeping in touch. Responses can be much more spontaneous and intimate even than written letters. The lack of formality of a hastily typed e-mail encourages frankness and honesty. If you have the chief executive's e-mail address, your message goes straight to the top. Before, if you wrote a letter, more than likely it went through an elaborate filtering process involving various flunkies whose sole job seemed to be preventing the boss from being disturbed. You'd be lucky if the boss even saw your letter.

And it works both ways. If you make something easier for people to do they will generally do it more often. If that chief executive thinks he can reply in just a few words that will take him half a minute to write, he's more likely to do so. Speaking personally, as an internet journalist for *The Sunday Times* I leave my e-mail address at the end of my weekly column. I gct a lot of e mails from company bosses who would probably not have bothered if they'd had to write a conventional letter. I also get plenty of useful e-mails from readers recounting their experiences. They probably wouldn't have bothered either unless they'd had e-mail.

> **TIP**
>
> *All the messages you've sent and received can be archived in separate files, making them easy to retrieve and organize. It is very easy to add senders' e-mail addresses to your address book. It also saves on paper and storage space.*

The speed with which e-mail can be sent means that service providers can keep in touch with their customers far more easily. They can tell you when they are running special offers, for example, or when your favourite shares have risen or fallen in value. Software companies can tell you when upgrades for their products are available, including links in the message to the exact page on their website. If you sign up for newsletters and online magazines you can have them delivered to your in-box every day. E-mail can be far more reliable than the paper boy or girl, ready to deliver your messages as soon as you start your computer in the morning.

When easier isn't always better

E-mail is so easy to use it may land you in trouble if you're not careful. It can be very tempting to rattle off an e-mail to someone when your blood is up and say something you regret later on. At least with traditional letter-writing you had time to cool off and think better of it. With e-mail, once you've pressed that **Send** button there's no going back – you can't change your mind once that digital rocket has been despatched across the network. So be careful.

Writing quickly can also mean writing thoughtlessly. Phrases meaning one thing and intended to be read in a certain way, can often be misinterpreted by the reader. E-mail can make it easier for you to give offence unintentionally, too. So before sending your e-mails, check them over first and apply the normal rules of letter-writing. Some people feel that because a message is electronic they can dispense with common courtesies, such as 'Dear ...', 'Yours sincerely' and so on. Some people don't even bother to include their names.

What do I need to set up e-mail?

First of all you need an e-mail address, normally assigned to you when you sign up with your ISP. Your address is normally based around your name before the @ symbol and the ISP's domain name after it. But don't assume that you'll be able to have whatever name you want. A lot of people with the same name as you may have signed up to the same ISP. If they've already bagged the name you wanted you'll

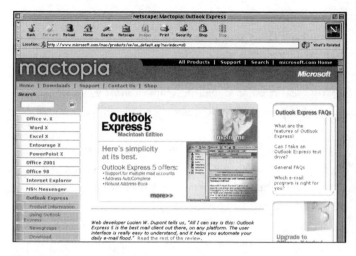

Two of the most popular e-mail programs: Outlook Express (above) and Eudora (below).

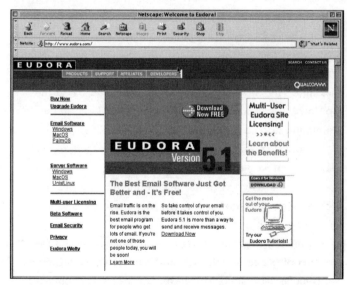

normally find that you have to settle for a variation on it, usually involving the addition of some numbers.

Sometimes it can take a long time just entering proposed user names into the registration box only for the ISP's server to throw them back at you because they've already been taken. If the ISP is very popular you can sometimes end up with an address that looks more like the code for an Inland Revenue leaflet rather than your name.

You also need an e-mail program or *mailer* – a dedicated piece of client software designed to handle all your e-mail messages. The good news is that such programs now come bundled in the Navigator and Internet Explorer (IE) web browsers. Navigator's mailer is called **Messenger** and IE's is called **Outlook Express**, or **Outlook** in the more advanced version.

As there are several different versions of these packages around there's not space to go through each of them in detail. If some of the instructions given in this section don't exactly tally with your version, look up the key word in the 'Help' section of your browser program. Unlike other Help sections in various software packages, the ones in mailers are pretty good.

You can launch the e-mail program in IE simply by clicking on the 'Mail tab' in the browser's menu bar at the top. In Netscape choose 'Messenger' after clicking on the 'Communicator' menu at the top.

Outlook Express and its enhanced version Outlook will also place an icon on your desktop. This is quite handy because it means you can just launch the e-mail software by itself, not the web browser, if all you want to do is send and receive e-mail at that time.

Fortunately these two programs are quite sufficient for most people's needs, although **Eudora** (**www.eudora.com**) is a popular alternative. There are plenty of others on the market too. You can research them at sites such as:

Download.com	**www.download.com**
Winfiles.com	**www.winfiles.com**
Dave Central	**www.davecentral.com**

Configuring the software

Mailers are pretty similar in look to web browsers. They have their own tabs and pull-down menus. To make the most of the features they offer it's a good idea to spend time browsing through them and getting to know them.

When you first load your ISP software that contains your browser and e-mail program, a set-up 'wizard' – automated installation program – takes you through the process step by step.

The main task when setting up the software is putting in the names of your ISP's incoming and outgoing mail servers. Your ISP will tell you what to enter in these boxes. It's usually something like 'mail.ISPname.net'.

The outgoing mail server is also called the SMTP server, which stands for Simple Mail Transport Protocol, the agreed standard for sending mail across the net. The incoming server is usually a POP3 server, which means Post Office Protocol. POP3 allows you to access your e-mail from anywhere on the net, even if you're online with another ISP.

You also need to enter your account name – usually the first part of your e-mail address. A common mistake people make when setting up the software is to put their full name in the 'Account name' box. For example, although my name is Matthew Wall, the account name for my e-mail address is actually 'mt.wall'. If I get this wrong the server can't recognise the name and won't let me get at my mail.

Another important part of the set-up process is the password. You don't want people being able to get online and rifle through your mail do you? As with all passwords, make sure you keep it secret. If you forget it, tell your ISP and providing you can pass some other security checks, such as your mother's maiden name, date of birth and so on, they'll remind you. The latest dial-up connection software allows you to store passwords on the system so that you can connect automatically when you launch the software without having to fill in any boxes.

Obviously this is more convenient, but less secure. Anyone with access to your computer could interrogate your e-mail in-box, read your mail, and worse still, send rude, career-damaging messages to your employers. Not a suitable option for the workplace then.

Writing, sending and receiving mail

The great thing about e-mail is that you don't have to be online to write messages. You can compose them at your leisure and then send several messages all in one go, saving online time and telephone bills. Just find the 'New Message' tab or its equivalent, type in the e-mail address of the person you're writing to at the top of the page, give your message a subject in the 'Subject' box, write your message and press 'Send'. It's that simple.

In Outlook Express this will automatically file the message in the 'Outbox' ready for sending when you next go online. In Messenger you just choose 'Send Later' from the 'File' menu. You can close down your mailer programs and come back to them later if you want. Your unsent messages will still be there.

To send them, go online and press the 'Send/Receive' tab in Outlook Express, or 'File', 'Send Unsent Messages' in Messenger. The latest version of Messenger shows a pop-up box asking if you want to send the unsent messages. To receive messages you simply click on the 'Get Msg' tab.

> **TIP**
>
> *You don't have to be online to write messages. You can compose them at your leisure and then send several messages all in one go, saving online time and telephone bills.*

In Outlook Express, clicking the 'Send/Receive' tab will also download messages into your 'Inbox.' If you don't want to receive messages yet, but just send them, you have to click on 'Tools' then 'Send'. This can be confusing because in the latest version of Outlook the drop-down menus only show those options you use most often. So the 'Send' option can be hidden. If you click on the chevrons at the bottom of the drop-down menu it reappears.

Once you've sent your messages they are automatically stored in a 'Sent' folder, which is a very useful resource. You can remind yourself what you actually said to someone before you write back at a future date. These sent messages can be sorted in several ways, too, including by name of recipient and date of sending.

When you receive messages you can read them straight away even while others are still downloading. Just double-click on the message and it will open in a new window. If you want to reply immediately, click on the 'Reply' tab at the top of the window and the sender's address will automatically be entered into the address box. You normally write above the text that was sent to you, although some people prefer to edit the quoted text and put their replies underneath. This is such a fast way of communicating that it's possible to have a near instantaneous discussion with someone, where each part of the conversation is recorded in the body of text below. Unless you change the title in the 'Subject' box, your reply will contain the same title with 'Re:' in front of it.

You can also forward the message you've received simply by clicking on the 'Forward' tab and then entering the e-mail address of the person you want to forward the message to. You can tell if you've received a forwarded message if you see the abbreviation 'Fw:' or 'Fwd:' in the subject line.

Building up an address book

You can store e-mail addresses and other contact information, such as telephone numbers and job titles, in your address book. The quickest way to add addresses to the book is to right-click on the sender's address. This opens up a menu of options. In Outlook you choose 'Add to Contacts'. This then opens an address book page giving you the option to add other relevant contact details and index the person's name in the way you want.

In Messenger, choose 'Add Sender to Address Book' and you're given a similar page to fill in. You save these and that contact is then added to the book. The advantage of this is that it saves time but also enables you to type just the name of the recipient in the address box, rather than the whole e-mail address. The e-mail program recognises the name and supplies the e-mail address for you – providing you type the name in the same way you logged it in your address book.

To add an e-mail address to the book from scratch in Outlook, go to 'Tools', 'Address Book', 'New', then 'Contact', or just click on the book icon in your e-mail browser menu. In Messenger, 'Address Book' is found in the 'Communicator' section. It calls new contacts 'Cards'.

> ### TIP
>
> *Over time your e-mail address book can become a significant and valuable resource. Don't run the risk of losing it if your e-mail software becomes corrupted for some reason. Save it to a floppy disk just in case.*

You can start a new message to one of your contacts in the address book in a number of ways – from inside or outside the address book. For example, in Messenger if you right-click on the contact name then choose 'New Message', the address is automatically inserted into the address box of the new message. In the Outlook address book, right-click on the chosen address, choose 'Action', then 'Send Mail'.

Back it up!

Over time, your e-mail address book can become a significant and valuable resource. Don't run the risk of losing it if your e-mail software becomes corrupted for some reason. Save it to a floppy disk just in case. In Outlook, choose 'Import and Export' from the file menu, then the 'Export to a file' option. You then have to select the format you want the file to be saved in – 'comma separated values (Windows)', for example. This doesn't much matter so long as you remember the file type you chose when you want to import the file back into your browser. If you get them mixed up you're likely to end up with a scrambled address book that's no use to anybody.

It does matter if you want to access the file from outside your e-mail program. Then the correct file format will depend on the software you have on your system best suited to reading these kinds of databases. A little trial and error is usually called for. But there's nothing to stop you saving the file in a variety of formats and seeing which one works best with the database software you have.

You then have to select the folder you want to export. In Outlook, the address book is the 'Contacts' folder. Click on it then choose a destination for the file – a:\Contacts Backup, for example, and then export the file. To import the file, you just carry out the same procedure in reverse.

The process is a little simpler in Messenger. Open the address book then choose 'File', 'Export'. Choose a destination drive and name for the file, plus a format, then click on 'Save'.

Sending mail to several people at once

Once you've chosen the main recipient of the e-mail and put the address in the 'To:' box, you can send the message to others by adding their addresses in the 'CC' (carbon copy) box underneath. You can put as many addresses in here as you like, choosing from the address book, or typing them in manually and separating each using a semi-colon. The main recipient will be able to see the addresses of all the people you've copied the message to.

If you don't want the recipient to see who else you've sent the message to, put their addresses in the 'BCC' (blind carbon copy) box. This is especially useful if you've set up large groups of e-mail addresses and you want to send a circular to all the members of a club, for example. There's no point clogging up the e-mail header with lots and lots of addresses unnecessarily. But everyone on the list can still see the name and address of the main recipient and anyone else in the CC box.

To prevent disclosure of anyone on the list you can put your own e-mail address in the 'To:' box and put the list in the BCC box. This can be a little confusing for some people because they'll see that the message is to and from the same person! At first it looks like a mistake ... but hopefully the contents of the message should make it clear that the message is for them.

WARNING

Bear in mind that if you receive a message as one recipient on a list, if you choose Reply To All your message to the sender will also go to everyone on the list. The ease of doing this in a hurry has led to some spectacular bloomers with private and sometimes indiscreet messages being broadcast to entire lists of people.

Creating e-mail lists

Your e-mail package can also help you to set up mailing lists very easily, which saves a lot of time if you're often sending messages to the same group of people. In Outlook, just click on 'File', 'New', 'Distribution List'. Give the list a name then select the people you want on that list from your address book, or add them manually. In Messenger, click on 'Communicator', 'Address Book', 'New List' and do the same.

Including a signature file

If you write a lot of e-mails you can include contact details with your message automatically every time you start a new one. It's a bit like attaching a business card and saves you typing out your details every time. It's called a *signature file*. In Outlook, start a new message then click on 'Tools', 'Options', then 'Mail Format'. Give your signature file a name then enter the details you want to include in the box provided. If you're clever you can create the file in a graphics package, adding colour and changing fonts, then import that file as your signature. But bear in mind that the more graphics you use, the longer it will take to send your messages. You also run the risk of alienating your recipients if it takes ages to download your fancy graphics file each time!

In Messenger, click on 'Edit', 'Preferences', 'Mail' and 'Newsgroups' in the file tree on the left, then 'Identity'. Messenger calls these signature files personal cards or vCards. You can include as much or as little detail as you like.

Sending attachments

W hen you compose an e-mail you can also attach other documents to your message, such as word processing files, spreadsheets, images and sound files. It's very easy. All you do is click on the paperclip icon in the mailer menu bar and then select the file you want to attach from whichever directory you've put it in.

When the recipient reads your message the attached file is shown as an icon along with the message. Click on the icon and the file opens. The only major problem you might encounter is that your recipient doesn't have the necessary software to read the type of file you've attached. For example, lots more people are using Adobe Acrobat for desktop publishing. But if you don't have the Acrobat reader software you won't be able to open these documents (called PDF files).

> ### TIP
>
> *Avoid sending attachments that are very large or in an unusual format. Many people resent having to wait ages for something to download – especially if they then can't read it.*

If possible, send attachments in a common format, otherwise you risk annoying people. You also risk annoying people if your attachments are very big – more than a few hundred kilobytes say. They take a very long time to download and it's their phone bill you're adding to. It's the quickest way to make enemies, especially if your attachment isn't even of much interest.

Another problem, thankfully now uncommon, is that the e-mail program you are sending to may be using a different encoding standard – UUencode or MIME are the two main ones – for attachments. If your programs aren't in sync your recipient will just receive a lot of gibberish. You can specify which standard your package uses. For example, in

Messenger's 'new message' window, click on the 'Options' tab. You can then tick a box if you want to use UUencode instead of MIME for attachments. In Outlook, click on 'Tools', 'Options', then the 'Mail Format' tab. In the box next to 'Send' in this message format choose 'Plain Text', then 'Settings'. If your recipient is having trouble reading your attachments, experiment by switching standards to see which works best.

Web-style e-mail

The latest versions of e-mail programs are very sophisticated, incorporating many advanced word processing features, such as a wide choice of fonts, cutting and pasting, and other standard formatting facilities. You can even create new messages as HTML web pages capable of containing links to websites and including web graphics and sound files. If the recipient clicks on the link from within the message it will automatically launch the web browser software and, once online, go straight to the selected page.

This is great news for advertisers because they can send you promotional e-mail and give you the exact web address where you can buy whatever it is they're trying to sell. It's an effective form of direct marketing. It's good for us too because we can decide pretty quickly whether we want whatever is being advertised and delete it or act on it in a trice.

Rather than including attachments with your messages, HTML e-mail allows you to incorporate pictures, charts, photos, sound files and video snippets in the body of your message by clicking on 'Insert' in the main menu, then choosing 'Picture' or 'Object'. Once you've inserted the selected file, you can then format it, making it smaller or larger, for example.

Managing your mail
....

If you get a lot of mail that you want to keep, it can soon become a headache trying to keep track of it all. E-mail programs are excellent at helping you organise your messages. You can create new folders easily and simply 'drag and drop' messages into the folders you want. Sorting them by date received, size of file, or sender's name, is easily achieved by clicking on the tab at the head of each column within the folder.

You can set up your program to filter your mail into various folders if you want, rather than having them all arrive in your in-box. But this is only really worth doing if you receive tons of mail. Look under 'filters' in your program's 'Help' section.

You can mark your mail as 'read' or 'unread' and flag it up to remind you to read it later. And when you're sending messages you can specify whether they are high or low priority, and whether you would like a receipt to prove that they arrived.

E-mail for businesses
....

Businesses that do a lot of e-mailing to long lists of people may need a stand-alone e-mail management program to help them. Here are some suggestions:

PC iMail	**www.prosoftapps.com**
NetMailer	**www.netmailer.com**
Campaign	**www.arialsoftware.com**
Mail essentials	**www.gfi.com**

Dealing with 'spam'

One of the disadvantages of making something easy to do is that it opens up new opportunities for life's undesirables. Included in this category are people who buy up huge lists of e-mail addresses then bombard everyone on that list with unsolicited mail usually of dubious value. One CD-ROM can contain some 60 million addresses.

This electronic equivalent of junk mail is known as *spam* and it has become a big issue on the net. It ranges from harmless attempts at mass-marketing to downright fraud, such as pyramid schemes promising quick riches and 'advance fee' scams. Some surveys estimate that spam is costing business billions and billions of dollars a year in time wasted dealing with it.

There's been such a fuss made, particularly in the US where privacy is a major issue, it has led to

> **TIP**
>
> *If you receive spam (unsolicited e-mail), don't reply to it – if you do, the spammer knows your e-mail address is in use.*

increased pressure on web service providers not to sell or divulge e-mail addresses, or at least to give surfers the chance to say whether or not they agree to the selling on of their personal details, including e-mail addresses. Some spammers have been banned by ISPs for jamming up their servers with bulk mailings and leading to a flurry of complaints from members. There are moves to outlaw the practice altogether.

At least with unsolicited e-mail it's easy to delete it quickly. But it can become annoying. There are some steps you can take to filter it out using your mailer settings, but these ruses are easy to avoid by clever spammers. The golden rule is never to reply to it. Until you do, spammers don't really know that you exist, given the high turnover in e-mail addresses. No response at all is the best response. Never let a spammer know where you live and if you are receiving indigestible amounts of spam, complain to your ISP – they might be able to block incoming mail from known spamming sites.

Sites such as Junkbusters (www.junkbusters.com) and Fight Spam on the Internet (http://spam.abuse.net) give advice and programs to help filter out spam.

Having said that – and I know this is tempting fate – I've written an internet column for *The Sunday Times* for over three years, leaving my e-mail address at the end of it each week, and I've not been troubled much by spam at all. So it's not an issue to worry about too much, just don't go giving your e-mail address away too freely.

For a plethora of information on spam and how to deal with it, including links to all the programs that can help filter out spam, go to **Junkbusters** (**www.junkbusters.com**), or **Fight Spam on the Internet** (http://spam.abuse.net).

Free e-mail everywhere

These days it seems that everyone is trying to offer us free e-mail addresses, from portal sites to search engines. They are mostly web-based services, called **webmail**, that you can access from any computer without the need to mess about with mail server address settings in the mailer program.

In fact you don't need a mailer program at all, you can access your mail from the web browser. All your messages are stored on the web, so it's ideal for people on the move. It also means that if you change your ISP you don't have the aggravation of having to tell all your contacts your new e-mail address – your webmail is independent of any ISP.

But there are downsides. For example, if you archive a lot of e-mail for reading offline, webmail isn't really suitable, unless you're prepared to stay online for long periods of time.

And with most of these free services you have to put up with online adverts cluttering up your screen. Another potential problem is that you are at the mercy of the web. At busy times of the day it can take a long time to access your account and access your messages. These services are truly international so they can have millions of people trying to access their accounts at the same time. With a local ISP the network loop will be shorter, and so you should be less affected by delays.

The most successful of the webmail services is **Hotmail** (www.hotmail.com), which is owned by Microsoft. It's so popular that getting the user name you want is difficult because millions of people have been there before you – it requires great imagination!

But it is handy having a back-up e-mail account if your ISP's mail service crashes, as it will from time to time. It is also useful if you want to be anonymous while on the web, because you can enter whatever details you like, including a

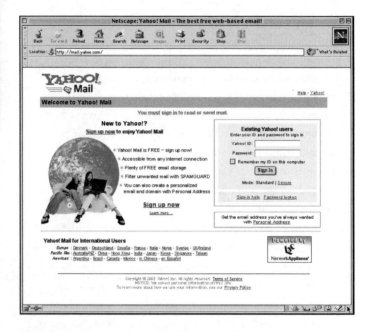

*Other free webmail services include Yahoo!Mail (above,
http://mail.yahoo.com) and Lycos Mailcity (below, http://www.mailcity.com)*

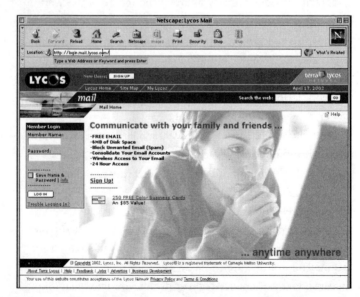

false name. Even this isn't a complete cover though, because it is still possible to identify you by tracing your computer's IP address.

Here's a list of some other free webmail services:

Another.com	**www.another.com**
Yahoo!Mail	**http://mail.yahoo.com**
Lycos Mailcity	**www.mailcity.com**
Net@ddress	**www.netaddress.com**
SuperNews	**www.supernews.com**
CoolList	**www.coollist.com**

For a more complete list try an excellent site called The Free E-mail Providers Guide (**www.fepg.net**) which has tons of information on over 1,400 free e-mail providers around the world. There's a country-by-country breakdown and tables giving the main features of each service. Another useful all-round site is Email Addresses (**www.emailaddresses.com**).

> **TIPS**
>
> *The advantage of a web-based e-mail account is that you can send and receive mail using any computer with internet access.*

Forwarding services

If you're happy with your ISP but you don't like the e-mail address they've given you, try a ***forwarding service***. You can get yourself a more exotic e-mail address and quote that as your main address to all your contacts. When people send messages to this address the forwarding service will redirect it to your ISP e-mail account. Again, this gives you the freedom to keep the same address no matter how many times you change ISP.

Some forwarding services include:

Bigfoot	http://uk.bigfoot.com
NetForward	www.netforward.com
Mail.com	www.iname.com

For how to keep your e-mail private and secure, *see page 241*.

Making the Most of the Web

Introduction to Part Two

In Part One we gave you all the tools you needed to get up and running on the internet. In this section we tell you how to make the best use of what the net has to offer. Whether you want to get the latest news or book a holiday, manage your finances or go shopping, the following chapters will tell you how and give you some great websites to visit.

Unlike other net guides, we haven't just listed all the websites that are out there, we've selected the best ones for you, so you don't waste time with the dross. If you're looking for a more comprehensive list of sites just bookmark a site like **UK Directory** (**www.ukdirectory.co.uk**). It lists thousands of categorised websites that are constantly updated and expanded.

If you're after the weird and arcane you'll find it pretty quickly on the web anyway – there's enough of it around. And if you want to see what all these other millions of surfers do with their time, go to a site like **Hot 100 Websites** (**www.hot100.com**), which lists the most frequently visited websites each week.

Chapter 7

News, Research and Education

Introduction

The net was invented and supported largely by academics wanting to exchange and share information. And this is still one of the net's greatest achievements. The sheer volume of information out there is awe-inspiring. Most newspapers are now online, as well as having net-only services, such as personal finance or technology-related sites. There are encyclopedias, libraries, dictionaries, museums and government departments online. Information, from weather forecasts to share prices, has never been so readily accessible thanks to this electronic medium.

Organisations have realised that they can save themselves a lot of bother by putting as much information on the web as possible, where people can help themselves without jamming up switchboards and wasting staff time.

The net can tell you what's happening this second via the many newswire services now available, as well as providing a valuable archive resource when you're researching a topic. What's more, the net allows information services to be much more interactive and users much more selective in what they receive.

For example, you can subscribe to any number of specialist online magazines and newspapers and have news delivered to your e-mail in-box. These services are often called *mailing lists*. You can pre-select the type of stories you're interested in, too. In fact, it has never been easier to keep bang up-to-date with events in whatever field you're interested in.

Just make sure that if you do subscribe to mailing lists you save the e-mail that tells you how to unsubscribe, otherwise you may find your in-box filling up even after several attempts at stopping your subscription.

TIP

If you do subscribe to mailing lists, make sure you save the e-mail that tells you how to unsubscribe.

Your ISP's home page is a good place to start looking for information resources. It's in their interests to make their pages and services as comprehensive and useful as possible. The latest versions of web browsers also contain lots of pre-selected links to radio, news and entertainment resources. These are sometimes called *channels*, although in my view, this attempt to make the web analogous to television confuses rather than helps.

Anyway, there are hundreds of news and research resources on the web, but here are some prime candidates for your bookmarks folder:

National newspapers

The Sunday Times	www.sunday-times.co.uk
The Times	www.thetimes.co.uk
Financial Times	www.ft.com
Telegraph	www.telegraph.co.uk
Guardian	www.guardian.co.uk
Independent	www.independent.co.uk

Daily Mail	www.dailymail.co.uk
Daily Express	www.express.co.uk
Mirror	www.mirror.co.uk
Evening Standard	www.thisislondon.co.uk

Specialist magazines and journals

Times Educational Supplement	www.tes.co.uk
Times Higher Educational Supplement	www.thes.co.uk
Times Literary Supplement	www.the-tls.co.uk
Primary Online	www.tesprimary.co.uk
The Economist	www.economist.com
The New Statesman	www.newstatesman.co.uk
The Spectator	www.spectator.co.uk
The New Scientist	www.newscientist.co.uk

Respected business journal, the Economist, offers both free and subscription services via its website.

News broadcasters

BBC	**www.bbc.co.uk**
ITN	**www.itn.co.uk**
PA Newswire	**www.pa.press.internet**
Reuters	**www.reuters.com**
CNN	**www.cnn.com**

The BBC's website is so packed full of news and entertainment resources it's like a mini-internet by itself.

News aggregators

BBC Monitoring (world news)	**www.monitor.bbc.co.uk**
NewsNow	**www.newsnow.co.uk**
Newswatch-UK	**www.newswatch.co.uk**
NewsHub	**www.newshub.com**

Technology News & Round-ups

Wired	**www.wired.com**
Internet.com	**www.internet.com**
NUA Surveys	**www.nua.ie**

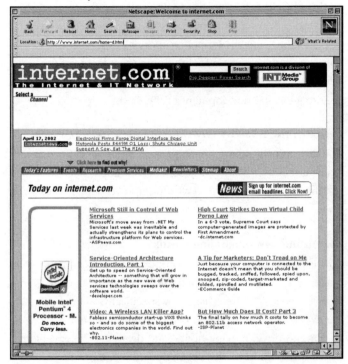

Keep abreast of technological developments with an IT news site like Internet.com. It offers a number of subject-specific e-mail newsletters you can sign up to.

Government information

The government aims to deliver all public services online by 2005 in a £1 billion push to get the UK online. Government departments are attempting to package the vast amounts of valuable data they hold for public consumption, as well as set up specific websites to promote certain government policies.

Here we list a few of the main gateway websites that should give you access to the major sources of official facts and figures, policy announcements and historical documents.

National Grid for Learning (www.ngfl.gov.uk)

The Grid is Tony Blair's ambitious plan to bring all aspects of education, whether formal or informal, academic or corporate, under one roof. He's hoping that learners, the education and lifelong learning services, and industry can all contribute to the development of the Grid.

Office of the E-Envoy (www.e-envoy.gov.uk)

The government set up a new post of 'e-envoy' in 2000 to oversee the 'UK Online' project. This is a good place to find out the latest news about moves to improve public sector online services.

UK Online (www.ukonline.gov.uk)

This is a new 'citizen information portal' that attempts to make public services more accessible and responsive to people's needs. Content has been specifically tailored around life events, such as having a baby, dealing with crime, learning to drive, moving home, and death and bereavement. New topics will be added regularly and the aim is to incorporate interactive services, such as the ability to register the birth of a baby online.

10 Downing Street (www.pm.gov.uk)

The Prime Minister has been leading by example with his well-designed site. It has colourful graphics, multimedia content and interactive elements built in.

The Public Record Office (www.pro.gov.uk)

The Public Record Office looks after all the national archives and has now redesigned its website to make it easier for researchers of all ages to use. It offers over eight million document references with plenty of links to other useful research sites, such as the Royal Commission on Historical Manuscripts. There's also a 'Virtual Museum' where you can find out more about the PRO and its 11th-century origins, and a site dedicated to helping you research family trees. Its '1901 Census' section proved so popular they had to remove it from the site for several months.

National Statistics (www.statistics.gov.uk)

For drier facts about births, marriages and deaths, population figures, and social surveys, the revamped National Statistics

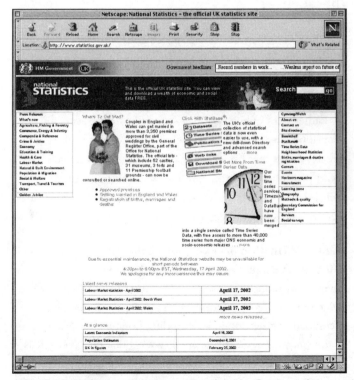

More statistics than you can shake a stick at from the Government's dedicated number cruncher website.

site is the place to go. It's not as user-friendly as it could be, but it's moving in the right direction.

OFSTED – Office for Standards in Education (www.ofsted.gov.uk)

OFSTED may be the bane of most teachers' lives, but its site is pretty useful for parents. You can find out how OFSTED's school inspection system works and read the reports for the majority of English schools in Adobe Acrobat format.

Online encyclopedias, dictionaries and thesauruses

In the days when the *Complete Oxford English Dictionary* can fit on one or two CD-ROMs – with all the space and cost savings that entails – it is clear that the internet is a perfect medium for reference material.

Rather than give individual web addresses for specific encyclopedias and so on, we've collated some excellent directory sites that list as many reference sources as you could possibly need. You can then scroll through each of their lists to find exactly what you want, bookmarking your favourite sites for future use.

BUBL Information Service (www.bubl.ac.uk)

BUBL is a catalogue of 12,000 selected internet resources covering most academic areas of interest. Search on the word 'reference' and you get a list of 74 reference works with accompanying descriptions, including popular favourites such as the *Encyclopaedia Britannica* (www.britannica.com). It is very fast because it isn't bogged down by annoying graphics and banner adverts – a breath of fresh air in this commercial world.

The 3W Virtual Library (www.vlib.org)

This is a truly comprehensive directory of resources, founded by Tim Berners-Lee, the British co-inventor of the web. It is maintained by cohorts of academically-minded volunteers. Just click on the 'General Reference' section for encyclopedias, libraries, dictionaries, lexicons, and glossaries galore. There are brief descriptions of the works, including the country of origin.

Xrefer (www.xrefer.com)

This is a search engine specifically for reference works, including dictionaries of quotations. It trawls through more than 50 reference titles containing 500,000-plus entries looking for your search terms.

yourDictionary.com (www.yourdictionary.com)

yourDictionary.com has collated some 1,500 dictionaries representing over 230 languages – the largest collection on the web. You can receive definitions in multiple languages and easily translate words into foreign languages.

Museums, libraries and art galleries

The British Museum	www.thebritishmuseum.ac.uk
The Natural History Museum	www.nhm.ac.uk
The Science Museum	www.sciencemuseum.org.uk
The British Library	www.bl.uk
3W Virtual Library Museums	http://vlmp.museophile.com

Schools, National Curriculum and Online Learning Resources

In these days of school league tables and supposed parental choice, parents have more information at their fingertips than ever before. Boning up on the best nurseries, primary and secondary schools to send your little darlings to is easy thanks to the web. All the performance data you could wish for is at hand. Not only that, but parents can have a look at school websites, too, and get more of a feel for the quality and ethos of the institutions.

Below is a list of websites that will help you choose the right schools, understand the education system and the National Curriculum, and generally prepare for launch on the schooling highway.

The Department for Education and Employment website is a comprehensive resource for parents and teachers alike, with access to school league tables and information about the National Curriculum.

**Department for Education and Employment (DfEE)
Parents' Gateway** (www.dfee.gov.uk/parents)
The DfEE has been very busy creating a number of new sites
designed to appeal to specific audiences. In the Parents'
Centre, parents can find out exactly what is being taught in
the classroom, how their children are tested, and all about
admissions policies. The resources are very wide and deep,
with information on everything from literacy and numeracy to
special educational needs. You can even find out about
school meals and check the address of your local education
authority if you like. Soon the DfEE will include links through
to all LEA websites as well. All aspects of school are covered
here, including related social issues, such as bullying, drugs
and truancy. It is a comprehensive resource that can only get
better and better as more links are included and more
interactive elements incorporated.

Schoolsnet (www.schoolsnet.com)
This education portal features a fairly comprehensive schools
guide providing information on over 22,000 schools, including
16,907 state primaries, 3,824 state secondaries, 455
preparatory schools, and 1,016 independent secondaries.

The Scottish Executive (www.scotland.gov.uk)
This umbrella site for devolved government in Scotland
contains the latest news about education policies and links to
other official Scottish sites.

Northern Ireland Network for Education
(www.nine.org.uk)
As well as providing links to educational establishments in
Northern Ireland, this site provides help for teachers, and
pupils from the ages of five to 19.

The Independent Schools Directory
(www.indschools.co.uk)

If you can't find what you're looking for in the state sector, there are always the fee-paying schools to consider. This useful portal site allows you to learn about and communicate with more than 2,000 UK independent day and boarding schools. You can also check which schools are offering scholarship and bursary entries.

BBC Online Webguide (www.bbc.co.uk/webguide)

Just click on the 'Schools' link of the BBC's awesomely comprehensive web guide and then bookmark that page immediately. There are links to hundreds of educational websites categorised according to subject and with information about the National Curriculum Key Stages that the sites cater for. A great starting point.

4Learning (www.4learning.co.uk)

Channel 4's education website is a well-laid-out effort organised intuitively according to the age group of the target audience. The online learning resources are closely linked to Channel 4's 400 hours of educational programming, including lesson ideas and interactive games and tests. There's also background material to the rest of its educationally relevant programming.

Learning Alive (www.learningalive.co.uk)

Learning Alive – formerly EduWeb – is an excellent resource for both teachers and pupils. It has several sections offering different services. For example, 'Pathways' is a database of more than 4,000 educational web pages searchable by age range, subject, or search phrase.

Topmarks (www.topmarks.co.uk)

This is a very good directory of websites for teachers, parents and pupils. It includes more than 1,450 sites selected for their user-friendly design and relevance to National Curriculum subjects. Searching the database is easy since the sites are categorised according to subject. The reassuring point about Topmarks is that it has been going for several years already and has consistently picked up plaudits along the way.

By Teachers is a website designed by teachers for teachers and brings together an impressive collection of online educational resources.

By Teachers (www.byteachers.org.uk)

By Teachers was formed in March 2001. It is a collection of educational websites that has formed an alliance called the Association of Teachers' Websites (ATW). Its aim is to promote awareness of just what is out there by way of free online teaching materials. It incorporates around 60 primary and secondary teaching websites.

Any website wanting to join the Association has to include high-quality teaching resources, be run by teachers, and be free to use. Perhaps crucially, new websites have to be approved by the other members of the Association before they can join. This kind of vetting by 'peer review' should ensure that high standards are maintained.

Early years websites

Words and Pictures
(www.bbc.co.uk/education/wordsandpictures)
Another BBC Education site aimed at children aged five to seven that ties in with the television programme of the same name. This one concentrates on reading and writing, exploring the building blocks of words, from consonant clusters to long vowel sounds. The site is clearly laid out with many interactive features.

Little Animals Activity Centre
(www.bbc.co.uk/education/laac)
This site is aimed at four- to eight-year-olds and includes maths and spelling games, plus an activity centre featuring recipes and finger puppet templates for children to download and print off.

Teletubbies (www.bbc.co.uk/education/teletubbies)
If you stay awake at night worrying about who spilled the Tubby custard, or you want to go counting giant rabbits with Laa-Laa, the Teletubbies site is a must. Although most parents have probably had enough of the 'eh-oh' cuddly aliens already, after a daily diet of the TV programme, the site does offer some fun interactive activities, such as colouring in online (no mess!). In fact, there are 120 online activities to

choose from, including teaching toddlers the difference between left and right. Bill and Ben never did that.

The Tweenies (www.bbc.co.uk/education/tweenies)
Kids can find out more about all their favourite characters, listen to the latest pop single online, and review Tweenies books on the site. Not overly educational, but probably diverting for Tweenies fans.

The Hoobs (www.4learning.co.uk/hoobs)
Channel 4's attempt to compete with the BBC's Teletubbies and Tweenies phenomena is the Hoobs – more cuddly creatures for pre-school kids created by Muppet man Jim Henson. They are intergalactic travellers who do a lot of discovering along the way. As well as a daily programme, the website features a dictionary and encyclopedia of the knowledge they have collected in transit.

Ladybird (www.ladybird.co.uk)
A beautifully colourful animated site from the well-known children's book publisher. The eponymous insect features large in the site design, making it an instant hit with children. You can find out about the latest books in the series and play online games, such as 'Incy Wincy Spider' and 'Bears and Balloons'. And then you can let the kids have a go! Some of the stories are online and there are sections for parents and teachers, too, with advice on how to read with children and use the site effectively.

The British Association for Early Childhood Education (www.early-education.org.uk)
Plenty of advice and teaching ideas for parents with pre-school and older children. You can download documents in Rich Text Format.

Revision help

The internet should never be thought of as a replacement for books, but it can be a useful supplement. There are several websites dedicated to helping angst-ridden teenagers cope with the trials of GCSEs and A-Levels as best they can.

BBC Education (www.bbc.co.uk/education/gcsebitesize)
The BBC's well-resourced and exhaustive education section covers most aspects of education. The site includes revision and test facilities in a whole range of GCSE subjects, from maths to design technology. For help with Scottish exam revision, go to the BBC's Scottish education site at **www.bbc.co.uk/scotland/revision.**

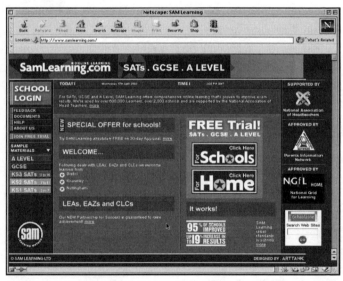

Angst-ridden pupils needing help with their revision can find it at sites like Sam Learning.

Sam Learning (www.samlearning.com)
A highly recommended revision site endorsed by the National Association of Head Teachers and the National Grid for

Learning. It provides 28 online revision courses covering SATs, GCSEs and A-levels. There's software integration for use offline and at school.

Some others to try ...

Project GCSE	**www.projectgcse.co.uk**
Learn	**www.learn.co.uk**
Revise It	**www.revise.it**

Further Education

UCAS – Universities and Colleges Admissions Service (www.ucas.ac.uk)

UCAS is the UK central organisation that processes applications to full-time undergraduate courses, HNDs and university diplomas. This site is a must for anyone considering higher education. You can search for courses that may interest you, as well as by institution and you can even apply to become a student online. UCAS also provides links to all those colleges and universities with websites.

Study UK (www.studyuk.hobsons.com)

This site tells you all about studying in the UK and about UK universities and colleges. There's a useful section on the costs involved, such as accommodation and travel, as well as views from students.

The Student Loans Company (www.slc.co.uk)

These days being a student is not cheap and many leave college saddled with debt. But if you need money, you need money. Find out if you are eligible for a loan, what the terms are, and how to make an application.

Sites for students

Gradunet (www.gradunet.co.uk)

After you've finished loafing around for three years and real life is threatening to bite you on the backside, check out this virtual careers office and look for a job. The site includes career advice and help on writing a CV that won't be instantly binned.

StudentUK (www.studentUK.com)

An excellent portal site just for students, featuring all the usual sections, from chat rooms to entertainment guides, sex advice and how to get stuff on the cheap. Let's hope most students are too busy working or having a good time to spend too much time surfing the web.

Cost-conscious students should make the most of free advice sites, such as Student UK.com – a fun and frank resource for feckless undergraduates.

Higher Education Students' Gateway
(www.dfee.gov.uk/hestudents/index.shtml)
Part of the Department for Education and Employment, this
site features several useful links for students, including advice
on how to get funding, apply for post-graduate research
places, and find employment in the real world.

Higher Education and Research Opportunities
(www.hero.ac.uk)
HERO is a comprehensive database of higher education and
academic research links for the UK. It features sections
tailored for people who work in higher education and for
students.

Student Unions (www.studentunion.co.uk)
An A–Z of student unions across the UK to stir those radical
bones in you.

Distance learning

Distance learning has been around for a long time,
fulfilling the needs of all those who may need extra
qualifications for career advancement, or who left school
without much to show for it. It is ideal for people who travel
about a lot or who cannot or will not conform to institutional
timetables or teaching methods either as result of work
pressures or by choice.

Here are some of the leading proponents in the field of
distance-learning courses, plus some information resources to
help you find out more about the subject and which
institutions have a better reputation than others.

Learndirect (www.learndirect.co.uk)

Learndirect is the government's initiative to encourage lifelong learning throughout the nation, to create a better-qualified, better-educated and more competitive workforce. More than 80% of the courses on offer are online, but there are also over 900 Learndirect centres where people can go if they don't have access to a computer. Most of the course materials can be found online, otherwise workbooks, CD-ROMs and videos can be sent to your home address. The aim is to make learning as flexible and as easy as possible. For the Scottish version of the site, go to **www.learndirectscotland.com**.

The International Centre for Distance Learning (ICDL) (www-icdl.open.ac.uk)

This is an amazingly comprehensive resource from an international centre for research, teaching, consultancy, information and publishing activities that is part of the Institute of Educational Technology. ICDL's distance-learning databases contain information on some 31,000 programmes and courses mostly in the Commonwealth countries, more than 1,000 distance-learning institutions worldwide, and over 12,000 abstracts of books, journal articles, research reports, conference papers, dissertations and other types of literature relating to all aspects of the theory and practice of distance education.

Open and Distance Learning Quality Council (www.odlqc.org.uk)

This is an independent charitable organisation set up more than 30 years ago to monitor the quality of distance-learning providers. It offers a 'rigorous' vetting and accreditation scheme and the site lists all the colleges it has accredited.

The National Extension College (www.nec.ac.uk)

The Cambridge-based NEC is a non-profit-making trust set up

to provide educational opportunities for all, not just those who got the right grades. It caters for around 20,000 students a year and there are 140 courses offered, including 26 GCSE subjects, 23 A-level subjects, and degrees from the University of London. There are also various vocational qualifications and business skills courses to pursue.

MindEdge (www.mindedge.com)

This is a slick US site set up by education professionals from Harvard and Massachusetts Institute of Technology. It is designed to be a one-stop-shop search facility for anyone interested in learning, whether online or via more traditional methods. It encompasses distance learning, continuing education and business training courses both in the USA and internationally.

Online universities
The Open University (www.open.ac.uk)

The Open University is the UK's largest university with around 200,000 part-time and full-time higher education students taking its courses. Around 40,000 students study interactively online. You can find out all about the undergraduate and postgraduate courses on offer, with advice on which course would suit your abilities and expectations.

University of London External Programme (www.londonexternal.ac.uk)

The University of London offers a wide range of diplomas and degrees online, targeted mainly at overseas students, with syllabuses and course materials available online. The University promises no drop in the usual standards of its qualifications, but there is no tuition offered. All papers are marked in London.

Unext (www.unext.com)

A US online university set up by leading academics initially targeting the global business market by offering employee training and business courses online.

Usenet: news and discussion groups

There is another resource on the net that no other medium can provide: other users. The other major part of the net besides the web is **Usenet**, the collective name for all the **discussion groups**, **bulletin boards** and **newsgroups**. When you download 'news' on the net, it doesn't mean news in the conventional sense, it's the collective name for newsgroup messages. By the same token, messages are often called 'articles' as well, just to confuse things further.

People can read and send messages to each other via these public forums, categorised according to subject. There are over 60,000 separately-listed areas of interest ranging from the erudite to the barmy. But they are open to the world and there is a wealth of opinion and experience waiting to be tapped if you know where and how to look. It's not just all text messages either, people can attach picture, video and sound files to their messages, too. You'll need all the right plug-in software to handle multimedia files though (*see Downloading Software and Files, page 67*).

When you're online to newsgroups you're not on the web, you're just talking directly to your ISP's news server. But you can also access all these newsgroups through the web, by going to sites such as those at **Google** (http://groups.google.com). This at least gives you more flexibility in that you do have access to the web as well, but you don't have as much control to organise your news messages as you do within a dedicated newsreader.

Of course, the volume of information can be overwhelming, so you need to marshal these resources carefully and be selective, otherwise you find yourself spending all day trying to read everything published, not getting any work done, and running up huge telephone bills. The net is very good at giving you the illusion of working when you're really just wasting time!

Usenet newsgroups are like public forums where you can post messages and read all the other messages. Anyone opening the newsgroup folder can read your message and reply publicly or to you directly by e-mail. Your messages could be read by anyone.

Setting up your system to access newsgroups

First you need a **newsreader** program. Luckily, the latest versions of Internet Explorer and Netscape Navigator include newsreaders that should be fine for most people's needs. Most ISPs have a dedicated news server, so you have to tell your newsreader how to recognise the server by entering its address. You may have done this already when you first signed up with your ISP. If you didn't, ask your ISP for help.

> **T I P**
>
> Usenet newsgroups are like public forums where you can post messages and read all the other messages. Anyone opening the newsgroup folder can read your message and reply publicly or to you directly by e-mail.

Once you've entered the name of the news server – usually 'news.ISPname.net' or something similar – you go online to download all the newsgroups that your ISP has stored on the server. You can then search for a subject you're interested in and 'subscribe' to that newsgroup, if one exists.

The discussion groups are categorised according to their content. The abbreviation at the start of the group name tells you the main subject area. For example, **sci**. stands for 'science' and **alt**. stands for 'alternative', meaning off-the-wall. As you move right through the newsgroup name you go down through subdirectories to more specific subjects within that category. So the longer the address, the more specific the subject. The newsreader search facilities are pretty good so you don't need to memorise newsgroup addresses. And once you've subscribed to groups they appear listed in your newsreader anyway. Just click on the one you want and it will take you there.

Reading news offline

Your phone bill can mount alarmingly if you stay online while browsing through messages. You can tell your newsreader to download all the messages at once when you go online so that you can log off and read them offline at your leisure without worrying about the bill.

In the Outlook newsreader, choose 'Work offline' from the 'File' menu before you go online. Choose one of the groups you've subscribed to, then right-click on it and choose 'Properties'. If you click on the 'Synchronize' tab you're given several options, depending on how many of the messages you want to download. Go online, click on the group, then choose 'Synchronize' from the 'Tools' menu. When you're offline again you'll be able to read all the messages you downloaded by selecting the 'Work offline' mode again. It's one of those things that's easier to do than describe!

In Messenger, go online and right-click on a newsgroup you've subscribed to. Select 'Newsgroup properties', then 'Download Settings' and set your preferences. Click on 'Download Now' and messages will be downloaded into your reader. Once offline, choose the offline mode from the file menu and browse away.

Posting a message

You can contribute to discussions or start a new one – known as starting a new *thread* – and also reply privately by e-mail. For tips on how to disguise your e-mail address when contributing to discussions, *(see Safety, Security and Your Rights, page 237)*. Give your message a relevant subject header to make it easy to identify. To start a new message, just click on the 'New Message' tab in your newsreader menu bar. You can send messages to several groups at once by putting them in the 'CC box' as with e-mail. Once you've sent a message you can also delete it from the newsgroup by right-clicking on it and choosing 'Cancel Message', but beware – the posting might still make it onto a few servers, and get read and replied to before it gets cancelled.

WARNING

Usenet users can be pretty intolerant of newcomers, so make sure you read the Frequently Asked Questions file in the newsgroup and follow the group's conventions as far as possible.

Following the rules

Avid Usenet users are pretty intolerant of 'newbies' – new users – coming in and flouting the conventions. So if you want to get along with everyone, make sure you read the Frequently Asked Questions (*FAQ*) file in the newsgroup if there is one, and make sure you have hit on the right group for the subject you're interested in. You don't want to waste people's time with irrelevant messages. There are a few no-nos when sending messages, such as typing in capitals – known as shouting – and being needlessly impolite.

Chapter 8

Shopping online

Introduction

These days it seems you can buy anything online, from novelty soap to luxury cars. Most things that you can buy in the shops, you can also buy on the net. It's only just taking off, and yet it's already massive. Not a week goes by without some research company coming out with another astronomical forecast for the amount we're going to spend online over the next few years.

What are we buying?

In the early days of shopping online we were understandably a little nervous about spending too much. The main – almost completely unfounded – fear holding people back was that their credit card details would be stolen and misused. So the most popular items being bought were books, CDs, videos, and computer software – relatively low-value goods that you didn't have to try out before you bought.

These days people are being a lot more adventurous – buying holidays, cinema tickets, cars, groceries, wine, clothes. You name it, people are buying it online. And as web retailers improve their sites and level of customer service, confidence is growing and the opportunities for online commerce are expanding daily.

Convenience is the main advantage of shopping online. The net never shuts, so you can shop online at 3am if you like. You don't have to worry about rushing out in your lunch hour and trying to buy everything you need before dashing back to work. No more struggling through traffic, arguing with traffic wardens or standing in bus queues in the rain. And what about that infuriating experience of battling through the Saturday crowds only to discover from some surly shop assistant that the very thing you want is out of stock? All that stress disappears.

You can do everything from the comfort of your own home at a time and a speed that suits you. There's a lot less pressure, apart from the niggling worry that you're running up a large phone bill as you peruse online shopping malls. But even this concern is fading as fixed-fee unmetered net access becomes the norm.

The net is especially convenient for those items that you have to buy rather than want to buy. Groceries fall into this category. Increasing numbers of people are happy to pay a premium for the added convenience of doing their food shopping online. Any parent who's dragged complaining kids round a superstore while being barged into by grumpy trolley-wielding grannies will fully appreciate the benefits the net can offer.

Cost

Although it's a mistake to assume that everything is cheaper on the net, many retailers are finding that they can undercut their competitors by offering goods online. After all, you don't need shops in high streets any more to reach a national audience. All you need is a well-designed website, a warehouse and an efficient delivery system. That cuts out a lot of the costs associated with running a traditional business. And this enables online retailers to offer lower prices to customers.

Books, for example, have dropped remarkably in price since online retailers Amazon and BOL entered the market offering discounts of up to 50% on bestsellers. High street bookshops, like W H Smith and Waterstone's, have been forced to drop prices in response. Such competition also accelerated their moves into online retailing.

Choice

The wonderful thing about the net's disregard for geographical boundaries is that a whole new world of choice opens up to the online shopper. Goods and services which might have been hard to come by in your local town are now just a click away. And we're not just talking about the UK. You can shop globally these days, buying from merchants in Singapore or Sydney, Manchester or Minneapolis. The net is opening up a truly global marketplace and there are lots of bargains to be found shopping abroad (*see Shopping Abroad, page 262*), even after taking VAT and import duties into account.

Is it risky?

No it isn't, not if you're careful. Shopping online using your credit card is a lot safer than buying things over the phone and certainly no riskier than handing your credit card over in a restaurant, say. The main fear – that your credit card details may be stolen and you could lose a lot of money – is unfounded. The misconception arises partly from a lack of understanding about encryption – the process of scrambling your card details according to a complex mathematical formula before they are sent across the network. This means that any hacker who was lucky enough to intercept your details in transit would be extremely hard-pressed to decipher the code.

Even then, your liability for so-called 'card-not-present' fraud is restricted to £50 in most cases, provided you haven't been negligent. And in fact, as long as you report any suspicious transactions as soon as you notice them, most card providers won't hold you liable at all. More and more credit card companies are now promising automatic refunds if customers are defrauded whilst using their credit cards online.

There are more legitimate concerns about retailers' own security arrangements and how they handle your personal data. But for more on this and how to shop safely and securely online, *see Safety, Security and Your Rights, page 257.*

The online shopping process

First, find an online retailer . . . There's lots of information on good places to start and excellent sites to visit later on in this chapter. Where you start largely depends on whether you know what you're looking for. You can go to a retailer's website direct, use a shopping directory, or try to find what you're looking for at an online auction.

It's quite usual to have to register on the website first. This usually involves giving your name, e-mail address and other contact details. So long as this isn't too onerous or intrusive, registration can be useful. It helps the website to recognise you when you return, and also to send you e-mails targeted at your particular interests.

You don't have to be online while filling in the form. Just log off until you've completed it. When you press the 'Submit' or similar button your browser should automatically reconnect you. If you still pay per-minute net call charges, this is a useful way of saving money on your phone bill.

Have a look at what's on offer . . . Retailers organise their products in a whole host of ways, some more logical than others. But basically you browse through an online equivalent of a mail-order catalogue. There are usually photographs accompanying product descriptions, although these can sometimes be very small. This is especially unhelpful on clothes sites, where you really want to get a close look at the materials.

One major advantage of the net over traditional forms of retailing is the amount of information you can supply with the products. For example, book sites often include reviews from people who've read the book you're interested in, or forums to discuss views on books with other readers. CD retailers will often supply snippets of music to help you decide whether you want to buy a particular album.

It's also very easy to search for what you want on the website. Most sites include a search engine so that you can just type in what you're looking for and it will take you straight there. This can save a lot of time browsing.

Select something to buy . . . If you find something you want to buy, you click on an icon that says 'Add to basket' or 'Add to trolley', using a supermarket analogy. You can usually enter the number of items you want in a box headed 'Quantity'. You can add as many separate items to your basket as you like while you're browsing. And if you change your mind, it's very easy to delete an item you don't want. At this stage you haven't committed yourself to anything.

Flash the plastic . . . Once you've finished browsing and you want to go ahead and buy, you proceed to what most websites call the 'Checkout' or something similar connected to the 'real' world. This is where you check that your order is accurate and that you've specified the right quantities. The site will usually work out the total cost for you, including delivery.

If you're happy to proceed, it's time to wield the plastic and enter your credit card details. Some sites will also accept debit cards. At this stage a website will often give you the option to go to 'secure mode', if you haven't been directed there automatically. Once you're in this mode, any data going to and from your computer to the retailer's computers is encrypted. Your transaction is safe from prying eyes.

You can normally tell when you're in secure mode when you see the web address at the top of your browser window change to begin https://. At the bottom of your browser window you should also see a locked padlock symbol. If you're scrupulous about security, you should never send your credit card details to a computer server that doesn't have an encrypted connection. I must confess that I have without suffering any ill effects, but I try not to make a habit of it.

Even at this very late stage you haven't bought anything until you click on the button saying 'Submit', 'Place order' or something similar. There's still time to change your mind if you get cold feet. But once you've clicked on that button there's no going back …

Order confirmation . . . Good retail websites will send you an instant e-mail detailing the order, as well as confirming it on the website itself. Make sure you keep this e-mail as proof that you made the purchase, and print off the website confirmation page as well just to be on the safe side.

Computers do crash from time to time and e-mails can get wiped, so old-fashioned paper-based back-up is a good idea.

Order tracking . . . Some websites will also let you track the progress of your order if you log on to the website. The correct web page address is often included in the e-mail. Again, it is good practice for the web retailer to e-mail you when the product is actually despatched, keeping you up-to-date with developments. Obviously, not all websites live up to these high standards of customer service and you should try to find out as much as possible about the company's policies regarding post-sales care before you buy.

Await delivery . . . After this relatively simple process, you then wait for your goods to arrive – hopefully accurately processed and on time. If you're buying from abroad, this can take several weeks. Domestic deliveries can take just a few days. The whole online shopping process can be extremely quick. I once researched and bought a new washing machine online in 15 minutes flat, saving £100 on high-street prices into the bargain. Of course, making a process easy can be a mixed blessing, especially if you're a shopaholic with a tendency to be profligate with your plastic!

A word about delivery charges

Some web retailers can be a little parsimonious when it comes to information on delivery charges. But it is very important. Any difference between online and high-street prices can be wiped out by the

> **TIP**
>
> *It's only when you click on the 'Place order' button that you actually make the purchase.*

added cost of delivery. So make sure you find out exactly what the costs are before committing yourself.

Obviously, the total delivery charge will vary according to the quantity and type of goods you buy. It is often calculated only at the very end of the process, once you've entered your card details. But as mentioned above, you can still go this far without committing yourself to anything. It's only when you click on the 'Place order' button that you actually make the purchase.

So if you think the delivery costs are too high, cancel the operation. One of the main advantages of the net is that there's no pressure selling. You're in control all the time and there's no queue of shoppers tutting impatiently behind you.

Web retailers have cottoned on to the fact that shoppers are concerned not only about product prices but also about delivery costs. Clarifying, or even removing, delivery costs certainly makes the whole process more straightforward. CD retailers in particular have felt compelled to consider this as they were facing intense competition from US retailers. You could buy CDs from the US more cheaply than in the UK, even after taking delivery charges into account.

Removing delivery costs in the UK helps to restore a level playing field. Music lovers may be tempted to spend a little more at a UK site if they know they're likely to get their CDs earlier than if they buy from abroad. When you make a purchase from a foreign website, true price comparisons are made more difficult if you have to include VAT and import duty in the equation. You don't always have to, but see *Shopping Abroad, page 262* for more information.

Price comparison services, shopping portals and directories

If you're not sure what you want to buy and you just fancy browsing, try a shopping-mall style portal, directory or price comparison engine for starters. These provide links to hundreds of other retail sites and often provide other services too, such as general security advice, shopping guides, and independent assessments of the sites on their lists. They are becoming more sophisticated in the quality of advice they give consumers.

Although there are stand-alone services around, more and more ISPs are incorporating shopping sections in their portal websites. Some ISPs and other service providers offer an added layer of security for their members by vetting retailers before listing them. They can often negotiate discounts on behalf of their members, too.

Some directories and shopping portals incorporate price comparison engines or agents into their websites. With these you enter the product you're looking for and the engine scans all the retailers on its list looking for the cheapest

> **TIP**
>
> *If you're not sure what you want to buy and you just fancy browsing, try a shopping-mall style portal, directory or price comparison engine for starters.*

price. Some include the cost of delivery in the price comparison, although none are sophisticated enough yet to work out the impact of import taxes as well. In time the number of product categories and the number of retailers and products within each category will grow and price comparison engines will become one of the most important services on the net. Anything that makes it easier to shop around for online bargains has got to be a winner. You won't need to go direct to retailers' websites any more. Price comparison agents also force retailers to become more competitive since any overpriced goods just won't show up in searches. Here are some of the best:

ShopSmart	http://uk.shopsmart.com
Kelkoo	http://uk.kelkoo.com

Two other popular shopping directories: Dealtime (www.dealtime.co.uk, above) and Bigsave (www.bigsave.com, below)

Pricerunner	http://uk.pricerunner.com
DealTime	www.dealtime.co.uk
Bookbrain	www.bookbrain.co.uk

There are also lots of general shopping directories that are a great place to start your online spree:

2020Shops	www.2020shops.com
Interactive Media in Retail Group (IMRG)	www.imrg.org
MyTaxi	www.mytaxi.co.uk
BTOpenworld	www.openworld.com/shop
UKPlus	www.ukplus.co.uk
Egg Shopping	http://shopping.egg.com
UKShopping	http://ukshopping.com
Bigsave	www.bigsave.com
I Want To Shop	www.iwanttoshop.com
Virgin Net	www.virgin.net/shopping
Yahoo UK	http://uk.shopping.yahoo.com
Freeserve	www.freeserve.net/shopping
Tiscali	www.tiscali.co.uk/shopping
Zoom	www.zoom.co.uk

Comparing prices abroad ...

If you want to see what's available in the US, there are a number of price comparison engines over there, many far more sophisticated in their breadth and depth than the UK versions. The best I've come across are:

BottomDollar	www.bottomdollar.com
MySimon	www.mysimon.com
PriceScan	www.pricescan.com
Shopper.com	www.shopper.com

Online Auctions

It seems that people are auctioning everything these days, from airline tickets to bicycles, fine wines to Beanie Babies. But it is the world of art and collectibles that has most naturally and successfully moved online. After all, an auction is the fairest way to establish the value of a work of art, since it has no fixed value in the same way a manufactured product like a washing machine does. And the biggest growth area is proving to be person-to-person auctions – a step up from classified adverts.

The net is perfectly suited to handling auction bidding, since it provides a single electronic platform for buyers who can be spread across the globe. It opens up new opportunities for people who may previously have been restricted to their local auctions. And it can handle the bidding for you even if you're not at your computer.

The so-called reverse auction, whereby surfers post a message online saying what they want and how much they are prepared to pay for it, is already a reality in the US and the UK through services such as **Priceline.com** (www.priceline.com and www.priceline.co.uk). This reverses the usual auction relationship since it is now the product or service providers who are competing with each other to pick up business. This kind of auction could have a massive impact.

How do online auctions work?

Registration

First you have to register, which means filling in an online questionnaire, giving personal contact details, and maybe a debit or credit card number. Remember that you should only submit credit details via a secure server that encrypts your details before they are sent across the web. You have to set up a user name and password so that the auction can identify you. There's nothing to stop you registering with as many auctions as you like.

Registering usually involves agreeing to the auction site's terms and conditions. These may look dull and it is tempting to skip past them, but you should find out about the site's charges and its payment and delivery policies before bidding. Some sites leave it up to the buyer and seller to sort out payment and delivery. And different sellers will have their own preferences.

Browsing the lots

Auction sites tend to organise their lots – the items up for auction – by category. Some specialise in particular areas, such as art and collectibles or tickets for events, but most cover a range of categories. You can browse through looking for anything that might take your fancy, or go straight to the category you're interested in, whether computer games or stamps. Most sites have a search box to help you find what you're looking for.

The lots are often accompanied by a picture and a description, plus any related information that may be of use. Sometimes the pictures are very small and it can be difficult ascertaining the condition of the lot for sale. The better sites will provide an enlarged high-resolution version of the picture if you click on the thumbnail image.

153

Two of the best-known auction sites are QXL (www.qxl.com, above) and eBay (www.ebay.co.uk, below) – Aladdin's Caves of potential bargains.

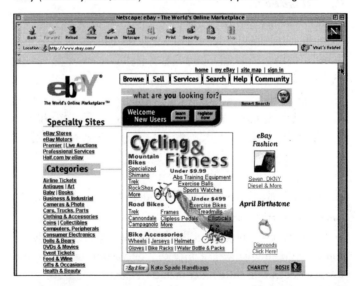

Placing a bid

If you like what you see and you want to place a bid, you have to log on, if you haven't already done so. This involves typing in your user name and password. Depending on the type of auction, you may then be allocated a unique number, sometimes known as a paddle. This is to identify you. There will usually be a box telling you the starting price for the lot, whether there is a reserve price placed on it by the seller, the latest bid, and the time remaining.

It may seem unfair, but you're not normally told what the reserve price is. Don't assume that it's the starting price – it's often higher than that. A low starting price is thought necessary to get the ball rolling. You just have to keep on bidding up until the lot shows the message 'The reserve has been met' or something similar. Even if yours is the highest bid, you won't win if the reserve hasn't been met.

When deciding how much to bid, the auction will usually specify the agreed bid increment. This is variable. It can be £1 for low-value items, but is usually around £10 or £20. You can simply type in the next highest figure into the bid box and press 'Submit', or the equivalent button. In a few minutes your bid will then be shown on screen as the latest bid. There's nothing to stop you making a *much* higher bid to scare off rivals.

You should note that if you win your bid, you can't just change your mind. You are contractually obliged to honour the transaction. If you have a change of heart and refuse to pay, the very least the auction site could do is ban you from using the site again.

Automated bidding

Online auctions can take several weeks, so the last thing you want is to be tied to your computer checking to see if anyone has outbid you. Luckily most sites provide an automated bidding facility. All you do is enter your bid limit – the most you are prepared to pay for the lot – and then the site's computer will place bids on your behalf until your limit is reached. It will only go up to your limit if people keep outbidding you. This gives you freedom to do other things rather than slavishly watch your computer. If you're successful in your bidding, you'll be told by e-mail. If you don't fancy the automated bidding bit, some sites will just send you an e-mail when someone places a higher bid.

Faster auctions

If you don't like all this hanging around, you can sometimes sort all the lots according to the time remaining. This gives you the option of choosing those lots that have only a few hours or minutes to go. This can inject a bit of excitement into what otherwise can be a fairly humdrum and long-winded process. It's also the quickest way to spot a potential bargain. If no-one has bid for a particular lot with only a few minutes to go, the chances are no-one will. You could nip in there at the last minute and snap it up. Bear in mind though that web auctions often reserve the right to extend the auction if there is intense bidding going on at the death. This may seem like moving the goal-posts, but there we are.

> **WARNING**
>
> If you win your bid, you can't just change your mind. You are contractually obliged to honour the transaction. If you have a change of heart and refuse to pay, the very least the auction site could do is ban you from using the site again.

Although most online auctions are spread out over a few days or weeks, they can also be live, with online bidders taking part in real auctions in an auction house. People in the room can be bidding against net surfers maybe several thousands miles away. This brings the excitement of the live auction room into bidders' homes. Some services even combine this with television for a true multimedia auction experience.

So far, such services are still in their infancy. We really need high-speed net connections to become the norm before live auctions take off in a big way. At the moment, the slowness and variability of net connections can introduce too many delays into what's supposed to be a fast-paced environment.

Delivery and charges

If you're successful in your bid, what happens next depends on the type of auction. For example, if the lot was sold by a company, it might have agreed to include the cost of delivery as part of the offer and take responsibility for delivery. With a person-to-person auction, it is often left up to both parties to decide how to take things forward.

As far as possible you should find out exactly what the delivery policy is and have a fair idea of the likely delivery cost before bidding. If the seller isn't willing to deliver, you may have to go and pick up the item, at considerable expense and inconvenience. You should also find out about other potential costs. For example, the auction site may charge a buyer's premium – typically 10% of the winning bid. There may also be local taxes and import taxes if you're buying from abroad. Most sites have useful 'Help' or 'Frequently Asked Questions' sections.

Placing your own auction advert

Most of the generalist auction sites allow people to place their own ads on the site for free, whereas some of the specialist art sites restrict this to affiliated dealers. Placing your own ad is simple enough. Once you've registered, you simply fill in an online application form giving details of the item you want to auction. Obviously the more arresting your description can be, the better. But avoid going over the top or you may end up in trouble with buyers and the auction site alike.

You can usually include a picture by attaching a graphics file along with your submission. You'll need a scanner to translate an ordinary photo into digital format or to take the picture using a digital camera. Look carefully at the site's guidelines if you want to do this, as there may be specific requirements for the size and type of file. Common graphics file formats are GIF, JPEG and Bitmap, but each site may have its own preferences. Once you've submitted your ad with a picture attached, be sure to check that the image has been properly loaded on the site. There have been cases of auction sites failing to do this correctly. As a picture considerably enhances your chances of attracting bidders, this part of the operation is crucial.

When filling out the form you're often given the chance to specify what payment methods you are prepared to accept and whether you expect the purchaser to pay for and arrange delivery. This all helps to avoid confusion later on.

Online auction sites

eBay	**www.ebay.com** or
	www.ebay.co.uk
iCollector	**www.icollector.com**
QXL	**www.qxl.com**
Yahoo! Auctions (UK)	**http://uk.auctions.yahoo.com/uk**
Amazon	**www.amazon.com** and
	www.amazon.co.uk
Loot	**www.loot.com**
eBid	**www.ebid.co.uk**
Priceline	**www.priceline.com**
	www.priceline.co.uk
Sotheby's.com	**www.sothebys.com**

| Artnet.com | **www.artnet.com** |
| Ubid | **www.ubid.com** |

Auction search engines and directories

Online Auctions	**www.online-auctions.net**
Bidfind	**www.bidfind.com**
Auction Guide	**www.auctionguide.com**

Shopping Abroad

There are some massive bargains to be had shopping at foreign websites. You can often buy CDs, books, and electronic goods far more cheaply from the US, for example. As a very rough rule of thumb, when you see dollar prices you can pay the equivalent amount in sterling, despite the exchange rate differential. This means savings of up to 30%.

And thanks to the net, it's very easy to do. Many of the shopping portals, directories and price comparison engines mentioned above have links to foreign websites.

But, of course, there are risks and disadvantages:

● Goods can take weeks to arrive

● Your consumer rights may be severely limited *(see Safety, Security and Your Rights, page 263)*

● If goods are faulty, getting them put right can be expensive and time-consuming

● Sometimes foreign specifications are not the same as in the UK, e.g. power supplies, video formats – you may be paying less but for an inferior product or one that doesn't even work in the UK

● Delivery costs, local taxes, import duty and VAT can sometimes wipe out any savings you thought you'd made

● You may not know anything about the website you're dealing with

● Not all foreign websites will deliver to the UK.

How do I work out the total costs involved?

Working out the sterling equivalent for the goods is easy enough. If the web retailer doesn't do it for you, use an online currency converter such as the **Universal Currency Converter** (http://www.xe.net/ucc).

When you come to the virtual checkout the retail site will usually work out the delivery costs for you, although these charges are often not very clearly described on the site. Sometimes you have to go as far as entering your credit card details and delivery address before it will calculate the total charge. You can usually opt to pay more for express delivery if you'd rather receive your goods in a few days rather than a few weeks.

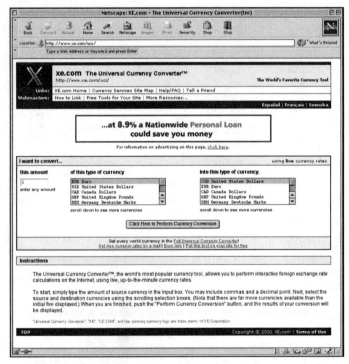

The Universal Currency Converter can perform instantaneous conversions in most of the world's currencies – a useful website to bookmark.

Depending on where you're buying from, there may be local taxes to pay. Then the fun really starts when the goods arrive at our shores.

Digital still cameras and computers are free from import duty, which is one reason why they can be much cheaper than in the UK. Books are also free from duty. And there is no duty on goods ordered online and delivered into the UK from anywhere within the European Union. Also, digitised products, such as software and music clips, that you download are treated as services by Customs & Excise (C&E) and so are free from duty. But you do have to pay VAT. And alcohol, tobacco and perfume always attract duty and VAT no matter where you've ordered from. Confused?

> **TIP**
>
> *As a very rough rule of thumb, when you see dollar prices you can pay the equivalent amount in sterling, despite the exchange rate differential.*

Customs & Excise, the government department responsible for all this, has a useful section on its website called 'Shopping on the internet'. Point your browser at **www.hmce.gov.uk**.

Site Guide

* * * * * * * * * * * * * * *

Some useful shopping websites:

Department stores and catalogues

Argos	**www.argos.co.uk**
Bloomingdales (US)	**www.bloomingdales.com**
Harrods	**www.harrods.com**
John Lewis	**www.johnlewis.com**
Macy's (US)	**www.macys.com**
Shoppers Universe	**www.shoppersuniverse.com**

Shopping.com (US)   www.shopping.com

Books

Alphabet Street   www.alphabetstreet.com
Amazon   www.amazon.co.uk
Barnes & Noble (US)   www.bn.com
Blackwells   www.blackwells.co.uk
BOL   www.uk.bol.com
Internet Bookshop   www.internetbookshop.co.uk
Waterstone's   www.waterstones.co.uk
W H Smith   www.whsmith.co.uk

Music, video and DVD

101CD   www.101cd.com
Amazon   www.amazon.co.uk
Blackstar (video
   & DVD only)   www.blackstar.co.uk
BOL   www.uk.bol.com
CDNow (US)   www.cdnow.com
CD Paradise   www.cdparadise.com
CD Universe (US)   www.cduniverse.com
HMV   www.hmv.co.uk
MVC   www.mvc.co.uk
Virgin Megastore   www.virginmega.co.uk

Clothes and fashion

Boden   www.boden.co.uk
Kiniki   www.kiniki.com
Cafe Coton   www.cafecoton.com
Charles Tyrwhitt   www.ctshirts.co.uk
Easyshop   www.easyshop.co.uk
Figleaves   www.figleaves.com
Freemans   www.freemans.co.uk
Haburi   www.haburi.com
Net-A-Porter   www.net-a-porter.com
Kays   www.kaysnet.co.uk

Redoute	www.redoute.co.uk
The Shirt Press	www.shirt-press.co.uk
Zoom	www.zoom.co.uk

Food

Abel & Cole	www.abel-cole.co.uk
Asda	www.asda.co.uk
Fortnum & Mason	www.fortnumandmason.co.uk
Jack Scaife	www.jackscaife.co.uk
Lobster	www.lobster.co.uk
Organics Direct	www.organicsdirect.co.uk
Safeway	www.safeway.co.uk
Sainsbury's	www.sainsburys.co.uk
Simply Organic	www.simplyorganic.net
Somerfield	www.somerfield.co.uk
Tesco	www.tesco.co.uk

Wine & beer

Berry Bros & Rudd	www.bbr.com
Laithwaites	www.laithwaites.com
Chateau Online	www.chateauonline.co.uk
Only Fine Beer	www.onlyfinebeer.co.uk
Virgin Wines	www.virginwines.com
Waitrose Direct	www.waitrosedirect.co.uk

Toys and computer games

Early Learning Centre	www.elc.co.uk
Hasbro	www.hasbro.co.uk
Games Paradise	www.gamesparadise.com
Gameplay.com	www.gameplay.com
Hamleys	www.hamleys.co.uk
Internet Gift Store	www.internetgiftstore.co.uk
Jungle.com	www.jungle.com
Lego	www.lego.com
Toyzone	www.toyzone.co.uk
Toys R Us	www.toysrus.co.uk

Computers & Software

Apple	www.apple.com/uk
Compaq	www.compaq.co.uk
Dabs	www.dabs.com
Dell	www.dell.co.uk
Dixons	www.dixons.co.uk
Download.com (US)	www.download.com
Egghead.com (US)	www.egghead.com
Hi-Grade	www.higrade.com
Jungle.com	www.jungle.com
Microwarehouse	www.microwarehouse.co.uk
PC World	www.pcworld.co.uk
Simply Computers	www.simply.co.uk

Consumer electronics and home appliances

Expansys	www.expansys.com
Argos	www.argos.co.uk
Buy Electrical Direct	www.bedirect.co.uk
Carphone Warehouse	www.carphonewarehouse.com
Comet	www.comet.co.uk
Dixons	www.dixons.co.uk
DVD World	www.dvdworld.co.uk
Go Digital	www.godigital.co.uk
Home Electrical Direct	www.hed.co.uk
Quality Electrical Direct	www.qed-uk.com
Richer Sounds	www.richersounds.com
Unbeatable	www.unbeatable.co.uk

Health and beauty

Academy Health	www.academyhealth.com
Allbeautyproducts.com	www.allbeautyproducts.com
Allpharmacy	www.allpharmacy.com
Boots	www.wellbeing.com
Pharmacy2U	www.pharmacy2u.co.uk
The Body Shop	www.thebodyshop.co.uk

Art & antiques

Artnet.com (US)	www.artnet.com
Axis	www.axisartists.org.uk
Art Connection	www.art-connection.com
London Art	www.londonart.co.uk

Flowers and gifts

Flowers Direct	www.flowersdirect.co.uk
Fragrance Store	www.fragrance-shop.co.uk
Interflora	www.interflora.co.uk
The Gadget Shop	www.gadgetshop.com
Thorntons	www.thorntons.co.uk

Travel and Holidays Online

The web and travel go very well together. For a start, getting from A to B, often via C, is a very complicated business. There's just so much information to deal with when you travel, from timetables and route planning to hotel addresses and foreign currency. Arranging all these separate components of a journey can be a headache at the best of times, especially when several of the elements are subject to sudden change.

Luckily, the web is particularly good at sifting and sorting vast quantities of data and disseminating it to the masses from one central, convenient place. Information can be updated very quickly online, making the web perfect for accessing the latest deals on flights and holidays, and news about disruptions to the rail network.

Holiday companies can advertise their wares more efficiently through a single website than via thousands of very expensive brochures. And online travel sites can aggregate all the competing holidays and trips into one place where we can search and compare all that's on offer. It's just so much more efficient.

This ability of the web to be bang up-to-date means that flexible travellers can pick up some fantastic last-minute bargains online. Travel operators don't mind because they can sell excess capacity more efficiently this way. It's better to get £5 for a filled seat on a plane than to have that seat empty. And technology has also helped introduce innovations such as online auctions, where people bid against each other, and reverse auctions, where people can stipulate the price they are willing to pay and see if the travel company accepts.

Is the web always cheaper?

Unfortunately, no. Although there are plenty of bargains to be found online and comparing and contrasting prices has never been easier, it's still a mistake to assume that prices will always be lower than you can find in your local travel agent or bucket shop. A high-street agent may have a strong relationship with a particular holiday company or airline and be in a position to offer even better prices.

So if you have the time and the inclination, a trip to the high street is still sometimes a good idea, if only to convince you that you're getting a good deal online. But the web is fantastic as a research and booking tool, saving you hours of time and trouble. That in itself can save you money. And in the broader scheme of things, by making it easier to distribute timely information and improve booking procedures, the web is helping travel companies to squeeze costs out of the system.

WARNING

Although there are plenty of bargains to be found online, don't assume that prices will always be lower than in your local travel agent or bucket shop.

Most travel-related companies have a website these days, from airlines to car rental firms, hotel chains to travel agents. There are hundreds and hundreds of sites out there and this guide certainly doesn't review them all. I've simply taken a cross section of the best to make your life as easy as possible.

Planning

How many of us arrive at our holiday destination completely stressed out simply because of the difficulties associated with organising the trip in the first place? We often feel we need another holiday to recover. In this section, I've collected all the resources you could possibly require to help you plan and prepare for your journey.

Timetables and ticket booking services

General
UK Public Transport
Information   www.pti.org.uk

Rail
Railtrack   www.railtrack.com
National Rail   www.nationalrail.co.uk
The Train Line   www.thetrainline.com
Transport for London www.londontransport.co.uk
Docklands Light
Railway   www.dlr.co.uk
Heathrow Express   www.heathrowexpress.co.uk
Eurorailways   www.eurorailways.com
Rail Europe   www.raileurope.co.uk
The Man in Seat 61   www.seat61.com
Eurostar   www.eurostar.com
Eurotunnel   www.eurotunnel.com
Amtrak (US)   www.amtrak.com

TrainWeb	www.trainweb.com

Ferries

P&O Ferries	www.poferries.com
Brittany Ferries	www.brittany-ferries.com
Hoverspeed	www.hoverspeed.com
Ferry Companies of the Web	www.ferrytravel.de
Seafrance Online	www.seafrance.com
Ferry Savers	www.ferrysavers.com
Eurodrive	www.eurodrive.co.uk

Bus and coach

Transport for London	www.londontransport.co.uk
National Express	www.nationalexpressgroup.com
Go-Ahead	www.go-ahead.com
Busweb	www.busweb.co.uk
Greyhound	www.greyhound.com

Travel guides

Newsgroups

One thing the web does very well is provide a forum for sharing individual experiences. These days you don't have to rely on the opinions of one or two jaded guidebook writers, you can browse through the views of real people in chat rooms, newsgroups and website bulletin boards. It's much more interactive and dynamic and you can gain a vivid insight into the places you plan to visit.

These newsgroups are categorised according to subject and you can easily browse through the subject headings using the newsreader program incorporated in the latest versions of internet browsers. A good place to start looking is the Usenet search site **Google Groups** (http://groups.

google.com), or simply open up your newsreader program and search the newsgroups listed on your internet service provider's server using relevant keywords. For example, there are several useful newsgroups in the **rec.travel** directory.

An increasingly common feature is for online holiday sites and guides to incorporate community bulletin boards on their sites, where visitors can post opinions and advice. It's a useful way to encourage people to come back to the site.

Search engines and portal sites

The internet search engine and internet service provider portal sites also collate some useful links for the traveller. They usually aggregate information and services from other holiday sites and companies.

Here's a list of useful planning resources:

Virgin Net	www.virgin.net/travel
About.com	www.about.com/travel
AltaVista	http://uk.altavista.com
Freeserve	www.freeserve.net/travel
Lycos	www.lycos.co.uk/webguides/travel
Search UK Travel	http://uk.searchengine.com
Yahoo!	http://uk.dir.yahoo.com/Recreation/Travel

General guides

Rough Guides	http://travel.roughguides.com
Lonely Planet	www.lonelyplanet.com
Concierge	www.concierge.com
Eurotrip	www.eurotrip.com
What's On When	www.whatsonwhen.com
World Wide Events	www.wwevents.com
Worldwide Holiday & Festival Page	www.holidayfestival.com

Guides to Britain

Britannia Travels	http://britannia.com/travel

Visit Britain **www.visitbritain.com**

About Britain **www.aboutbritain.com**

Brochures

Holiday Wizard **www.holidaywizard.co.uk**

Route planners

Automobile Association

www.theaa.com

RAC **www.rac.co.uk**

Green Flag **www.greenflag.co.uk**

Michelin **www.michelin-travel.com**

PetrolBusters.com **www.petrolbusters.com**

Maps

Mapquest (US) **www.mapquest.com**

Multimedia Mapping **www.multimap.com**

Map Machine **www.nationalgeographic.com/resources/ngo/maps**

Maps.com **www.maps.com**

Weather

Meteorological Office **www.met-office.gov.uk**

AccuWeather **www.accuweather.com**

Learning the lingo

Learning a few phrases of the local lingo is always a good idea before you travel abroad, if only to get you out of a tight spot in an emergency. Of course, the pocket dictionary will come in handy for such essential phrases as 'my postilion has been struck by lightning', but the web can be handy for self-help lessons before setting off.

Fodor's Living Language **www.fodors.com/language**

Travlang **www.travlang.com**

Health and safety information

Now that modern technology has given us the opportunity to travel to far-flung places around the globe, we also have the chance to contract some really interesting diseases into the bargain. Knowing what jabs to have and what health precautions to take is obviously important. Luckily, there are a few excellent advice sites around to keep us healthy while on holiday.

Fit For Travel **www.fitfortravel.scot.nhs.uk/Home.html**
Department of Health **www.doh.gov.uk/traveladvice**
The Foreign Office **www.fco.gov.uk**

Passports

UK Passport Agency **www.ukpa.gov.uk**

Travelling with pets

Pet Travel Scheme
http://www.defra.gov.uk/animalh/quarantine/index.htm

The Department for Environment, Food, and Rural Affairs website tells you everything you need to know about getting your pet microchipped for identification purposes when travelling abroad under the new Pet Travel Scheme. You also have to see that your pet is vaccinated and has a blood test before setting off. Plus, there's advice on how to look after your pet in transit.

Flights

Researching and booking flights is the most popular travel-related activity on the web. Airlines, especially the discount operations, are finding that the web is a powerful tool for selling seats at low cost. Ryanair and easyJet have been trouncing the main carriers recently. The world of airline seats is a complicated one. You'd think that a seat on a

173

plane came at a set price. Not so. It's quite common for two people to be sitting next to each other on the same flight having paid radically different amounts. We don't need to go into all the ins and outs of the business here, but suffice it to say that in such a fluid market dictated by the laws of supply and demand, it pays to shop around and be flexible in your travel arrangements.

With so many airlines competing for so many routes and schedules, the web has become the perfect tool for interrogating massive 'real-time' databases, for the industry and the travelling public. The most common flight specialists on the web are so-called consolidators – companies that buy blocks of seats from the airlines then try to sell them on to us. But almost all travel websites contain a flights section these days.

In this section there are lots of flight-related web resources, including airports and airlines, online travel agents and flight auction sites, with tips on how to find the cheapest fares around.

Airports

BAA	**www.baa.co.uk**
A2bAirports	**www.a2bairports.com**
Airwise Airport Guide	
	http://www.airwise.com/airports/index.html

Airlines

Airlines of the Web	**www.flyaow.com**
A2Btravel.com	**www.a2btravel.com/airlines.html**
British Airways	**www.british-airways.com**
British Midland	**www.flybmi.com**
Virgin Atlantic	**www.virgin-atlantic.com**
United Airlines	**www.ual.com**

Discount airlines

Go!	**www.go-fly.com**

Virgin Express	**www.virgin-express.com**
easyJet	**www.easyjet.com**
Ryanair	**www.ryanair.com**
Buzz	**www.buzzaway.com**

Flight sites

This is where it gets complicated. For a start, there are myriad travel sites out there offering flights. The choice is bewildering. Some simply publish all the quoted airline fares, others specialise in rooting out last-minute bargains. The flight prices themselves are often wrapped up in ribbons of conditions. For example, you may find that special offer tickets have to be bought at least five days in advance or are not available at weekends.

WARNING

Bear in mind that in many cases quoted fares won't include airport taxes. These can take the shine off an apparent bargain pretty quickly.

There's no single easy way to find cheap fares, because there are so many variables involved in reaching the final price you see on screen. What's more, the price you see isn't necessarily the price you'll get. It all depends on what day and what time you want to travel.

But the great thing about using an online flight agent is that it does most of the shopping around for you. If you go direct to an airline you can never be sure you're getting the best price. Then again, not all the online agents will have access to all the available prices. So it pays to try several online agents and go direct as well, just to make sure.

If you follow our checklist at the end of this section you'll have a good chance of landing yourself some decent bargains.

Expedia	**www.expedia.co.uk**	175

Travelocity	**www.travelocity.co.uk**
Ebookers	**www.ebookers.com**
Cheapflights	**www.cheapflights.com**
Dial-A-Flight	**www.dialaflight.com**
Lastminute.com	**www.lastminute.com**
Bargainholidays	**www.bargainholidays.com**
Deckchair	**www.deckchair.com**
Just The Ticket	**www.justtheticket.co.uk**
Air Tickets Direct	**www.booking.airtickets.co.uk**
Sky Deals	**www.skydeals.co.uk**
Airline Network	**www.airnet.co.uk**
Discount Holidays and Flights	**www.dhf.co.uk**

Cheap and cheerful

International Association of
Air Travel Couriers (UK) **www.aircourier.co.uk**

If you don't mind doing a little bit of work in return for massive savings on scheduled courier flights, then joining the IAATC is worthwhile. The courier usually carries a small package of documents but also has the normal baggage allowance. Discounts of up to 75% are possible.

Flight auctions

You can sometimes find some flight bargains if you're prepared to bid against other travellers at online auctions. Just make sure you know what the terms and conditions are before you pitch. Have a look at some of the auction sites listed in the chapter on shopping online (*see page 158*).

A new twist on the auction concept is the so-called reverse auction. Instead of bidders competing against each other, you indicate a price you are prepared to pay and then wait to see if any provider is willing to take you up on your offer. It originated in the USA, of course, but is beginning to gain a foothold in the UK, largely thanks to its main proponent, **Priceline** (**www.priceline.co.uk**).

All you do is decide how much you are prepared to pay for a particular flight, enter it on the website or ring Priceline's freephone number (0800 074 5000), and it then interrogates the airlines to see if there are any takers.

Of course, the difficulty with this kind of reverse auction process is that you have to decide what you think a flight is worth. That's no easy task. Bid too low, and you'll just waste time as no-one will take you up on the offer. Bid too high and you run the risk of paying over the odds.

When you bid for a ticket you have to give your credit card details at the same time, so there's no changing your mind once your offer has been accepted. And although you enter the dates and times you want to travel when bidding, you won't

> **WARNING**
>
> *Before you commit yourself to the bidding process in an auction, check out the conditions. You may find that you can't travel at a convenient time, or you may have to stay a certain number of nights.*

necessarily get the time or date you want, so flexibility is required.

Cheap fares checklist

❶ First check the websites of the airline companies that fly to your destination. They may have time-limited special offers on certain destinations.

❷ Compare this price with those offered by discount travel agents.

❸ Then check the direct-selling discount airlines.

❹ Also try the general online holiday agents, such as Bargainholidays.

❺ You may strike it lucky with an auction site, such as eBay.

❻ Find out the relevant airport taxes for your journey and make sure you know whether the quoted price includes these.

❼ Take 40% from the cheapest fare you can find then make a bid on Priceline at this level. You've got nothing to lose and a bargain fare to gain. Bear in mind that Priceline bids are pre-tax and and they'll add a £5 handling charge on top.

Accommodation

In this section we look at booking hotels, bed & breakfasts, hostels and any other type of accommodation you can think of. Whether you fancy a long weekend in a chocolate-box cottage in the Cotswolds or a couple of nights in a romantic Parisian hotel, we give you the websites that can fulfil your desires most efficiently.

Hotel chains

International chains

Hilton Hotels	www.hilton.com
Sheraton	www.sheraton.com
Holiday Inn	www.holiday-inn.com
Radisson Hotels	www.radisson.com
Crowne Plaza	http://www.basshotels.com/crowneplaza
Four Seasons	www.fourseasons.com
Hyatt	www.hyatt.com
Inter-Continental	www.interconti.com
Le Méridien	www.lemeridien-hotels.com
Mandarin Oriental	www.mandarin-oriental.com

| Accor | www.accor.com |
| Marriott International | www.marriott.com |

UK chains

Britannia	www.britanniahotels.com
Moat House Hotels	www.moathousehotels.co.uk
Posthouse	www.posthouse-hotels.co.uk
Jarvis	www.jarvis.co.uk
The Savoy Group	www.savoy-group.co.uk
Swallow Hotels	www.swallowhotels.com
Thistle	www.thistlehotels.com
Travelodge	www.travelodge.co.uk
Travelinn	www.travelinn.co.uk

Hotel finders

These websites attempt to provide an all-round accommodation service, finding you somewhere to stay at hundreds of hotels, B&Bs and hostels around the world. There isn't one service that covers absolutely everything – yet. As ever, you will have to try several to get a feel for what's out there in the area you want to stay and at the price you can afford.

International

Hotel Guide	www.hotelguide.com
Accommodation Search Engine	www.ase.net
Places To Stay	www.placestostay.com
Hotelstravel.com	www.hotelstravel.com
Hotel Discounts	www.hoteldiscount.com
CnGHotels	www.cnghotels.com
Laterooms	www.laterooms.com
Need A Hotel	www.needahotel.com
All Hotels	www.all-hotels.com
Hotel World Guide	www.hotelworld.com
Hotelnet	www.hotelnet.co.uk

Holiday-Rentals.com   **www.holiday-rentals.co.uk**

UK-specific

Most of the hotel-finder sites above contain UK-specific sections, but there are a number of UK specialist sites that go into more depth. Here are some of the best.

The AA Hotel Guide	**http://www.theaa.com/ getaway/hotels/hotels _home.jsp**
A2Btravel	**www.a2btravel.com/ accommodation.html**
Hotelmaster	**www.hotelmaster.co.uk**
Country House Hotels	**www.country-house- hotels.com**
B&B My Guest	**www.beduk.co.uk**
Tucked Up	**www.tuckedup.com**
Fairhaven Holiday Cottages	**www.fairhaven- holidays.co.uk**
English Country Cottages	**www.english-country- cottages.co.uk**
Internet Cottages	**www.internet-cottages.com**
The National Trust Cottages	**www.nationaltrust.org.uk/ cottages**
Pets On Holiday	**www.pets-on-holiday.com**

Hostels

At the budget end of the scale, hostels can provide cheap, reasonable accommodation for travellers more interested in a good night's sleep than the merits of the minibar.

Hostels.com	**www.hostels.com**
Youth Hostels Association	**www.yha.org.uk**

Camping and caravanning

For those who really want to get close to nature, tents and caravans are the only form of accommodation worth

bothering with. Try these sites for places to pitch up and boil
the billycan:

European Camping Index	**www.oginet.com/camping**
USA Camp Sites	**www.usacampsites.com**
Eurocamp	**www.eurocamp.co.uk**
Keycamp	**www.keycamp.co.uk**
Camping France	**www.campingfrance.co.uk**
UK Camping and Caravanning Directory	**www.camping.uk-directory.com**
Caravan SiteFinder UK	**www.caravan-sitefinder.co.uk**

Home exchange

One unusual, but increasingly popular, way of organising a
holiday on the cheap without necessarily compromising on
the level of accommodation, is home exchange. Basically, you
swap houses for a few weeks with people who want to come
to your country. You get to stay for free in – hopefully – an
interesting and characterful property with none of the
artificiality and superficiality associated with some bland
hotels. You're more likely to be based in the heart of a
community rather than banished to some roundabout at the
edge of a city's ring road.

You obviously have to feel you can trust the people you
loan your own house to, and there are insurance
considerations to take into account. This level of trust takes
time to build up and is usually established through regular
communication by e-mail or phone. Home exchange websites
resemble communities of like-minded people for this reason.
With most sites you have to become a member.

The websites act as agents bringing interested parties
together. You advertise your property online (typical cost
£20), including pictures where possible, and peruse the
adverts left by other home exchangers. The system works
particularly well for families wanting to travel long distances,

where a 100% saving on the accommodation could make a big difference to the total cost of the holiday.

Here are some leading home exchange sites to check out:

International Home Exchange Network	**www.homexchange.com**
Homelink International	**www.homelink.org.uk**
Exchanges Worldwide	**www.exchangesworldwide.com**
Home Exchange Vacations	**www.homebase-hols.com**
Latitudes Home Exchange	**www.home-swap.com**

Car rental

Car rental may sound straightforward, but it can be tricky. You have to know exactly where and when you want to pick up the car and where and when you'll return it. Not all companies will allow you to return the car to a different location, or to a location that suits you, rather than direct to the rental company.

WARNING

Insurance policies can vary markedly from company to company. Remember to check the smallprint.

Luckily, the web is making it easier to plan journeys and book cars in locations all round the world. Most of the major rental companies now offer booking online, and almost all the holiday agent websites include a car rental section.

Car rental companies

Avis Car Rental	**www.avis.com**
Hertz Car Rental	**www.hertz.com**
Europcar	**www.europcar.com**
Thrifty Car Rentals	**www.thrifty.co.uk**

| easycar | www.easycar.com |
| Budget Rent-A-Car | www.drivebudget.com |

Comparison services

Travelocity	www.travelocity.co.uk
Holiday Autos	www.holidayautos.co.uk
Rentadeal.com	www.rentadeal.com
Ebookers	www.ebookers.com/travelagent/cars

Holidays

It seems that the whole travel industry has moved online, from tour operators to travel agents. Categorising all these sites is difficult given that many attempt to be all things to all people, including all types of holiday and all types of travel-related service on their sites. Other sites stick to what they think they're good at, whether that's skiing holidays or cruises. As ever, you'll have to check out quite a few sites to find your ideal holiday, but daydreaming about escape to sunnier climes doesn't seem to be the most onerous of chores. The more flexible you are prepared to be with your destination and time of travel, the more likely it is you'll find a bargain.

Tour operators and holiday companies

The Association of Independent Tour Operators	www.aito.co.uk
Airtours	www.airtours.com
Thomson Holidays	www.thomson-holidays.com
JMC	www.holidays.jmc.com
First Choice	www.firstchoiceholidaysplc.com

Travel agents

| Thomas Cook | www.thomascook.com |

Lunn Poly	**www.lunnpoly.com**
My Travel	**www.mytravel.com**
Realholiday	**www.realholiday.co.uk**
A2Btravel.com	**www.a2btravel.com**
Online Travel Company	**www.otcuk.com**
The First Resort	**www.firstresort.com**
Holiday Bank	**www.holidaybank.co.uk**
The Independent Traveller	
	www.independenttraveller.co.uk
Holiday Shopping Guide	**www.holiday.beeb.com**
A1 Flights and Holidays	**www.a1fah.co.uk**
STA Travel	**www.statravel.co.uk**
Teletext	**www.teletext.co.uk**
Expedia	**www.expedia.co.uk**
Ebookers	**www.ebookers.com**
Holiday Rentals	**www.holiday-rentals.co.uk**

Last-minute bargain specialists

If you're footloose and fancy-free and ready to pack your bags at the drop of a hat, there are some great last-minute holiday deals available on the web. Your place in the sun is just a few mouse-clicks away ... and a telephone call, usually.

The last-minute bargain hunter shouldn't be too picky about destination or accommodation. One thing websites seldom show you is what your hotel or apartment looks like. In fact, the lack of accommodation photos is a serious failing on many of the package holiday travel sites. And bear in mind that with some very late bookings, you're not even allocated accommodation until you get there.

> **TIP**
>
> *Make sure you have a rough idea about the usual cost of the holiday to help you decide whether or not you are really bagging a bargain before committing yourself.*

You have to move quickly, too. Although the web is excellent at conveying up-to-the-second information, last-minute deals can go very quickly – sometimes even while you're browsing the site! So if you spot something that takes your fancy, leap at it straight away. There's nothing more annoying than making up your mind to be impulsive only to find that there are no seats left of the plane you want to travel on. Also, the usual condition attached to this kind of special offer is that you don't get a refund if you cancel.

Many of the holiday sites already mentioned above also include 'last-minute' and 'late-availability' offers on their sites. In fact, you may begin to suspect that holiday companies and travel agents use these tags as a bit of a marketing gimmick, knowing what suckers we are for a bargain. Occasionally the 'last-minute' prices on some flights and holidays don't look too different from those with departure dates that are months away.

As ever, it pays to be wary and shop around. The sites listed below make a feature of offering this kind of discounted deal.

Lastminute.com	**www.lastminute.com**
Bargainholidays	**www.bargainholidays.com**
Travelchoice	**www.travelchoice.co.uk**
Go-nowtravel.com	**www.go-nowtravel.com**
Global Travel	**www.globalholidays.co.uk**
Late Deals	**www.latedeals.co.uk**

Holidays in Britain

Visit Britain	**www.visitbritain.com**
About Britain	**www.aboutbritain.com**
Walking Britain	**www.walkingbritain.co.uk**
Britain Express	**www.britainexpress.com**

Skiing holidays

Skiing requires a section all of its own, primarily because it is so popular – around a million people in this country actually seem to like it – and because there are so many ski-related websites dedicated to bringing pistes to all mankind. Luckily I don't attempt to name them all here, but I do select some of the leading contenders in a rapidly expanding market.

1Ski	www.1ski.com
Ski Holidays	www.ski-holidays.com
IfYouSki	www.ifyouski.com
Iglu	www.iglu.com
Rocket Ski	www.rocketski.com
The Ski Club of Great Britain	www.skiclub.co.uk
Ski Esprit	www.ski-esprit.co.uk
Family Ski Company	www.familyski.co.uk

Other activity holidays

Adventure Directory	www.adventuredirectory.com
Travel with Bicycles	www.bikeaccess.net/default.cfm
Unmissable	www.unmissable.com
Travelchest	www.travelchest.co.uk
Voyages Jules Verne	www.vjv.co.uk

Cruises

Just like skiing, cruises are a whole holiday sub-category on their own. There are so many options available and so many operators specialising in them that aggregator websites make sense for most people, unless you insist on sailing on the QE2, of course.

Ecruise	www.ecruise.co.uk
Cunard Line	www.cunardlines.co.uk
Cruise	www.cruise.com

Foreign currency

Buying foreign currency and traveller's cheques is usually the last thing on our minds when organising a trip or holiday. We often leave it to the last minute and end up being fleeced with poor exchange rates at airport bureaux de change. These days the need to take cash or TCs with us is far less pressing thanks to the growing network of cash machines around the world and the extension of international network agreements between card companies.

But if you like the security of cash in your back pocket (sensible if the only cash machine in the mountain village doesn't work) then the web can help you order your currency quickly and efficiently. Why waste time queuing in a bank or post office when you can have it delivered for a small fee?

Below we give you some online foreign currency vendors to look at. Be sure to compare exchange rates and delivery charges before flashing the plastic.

Thomas Cook	**www.thomascook.co.uk**
OnlineFX	**www.onlinefx.co.uk**
SimplyFX	**www.simplyfx.com**

ATM locations

Visa	**http://international.visa.com/ps**
Mastercard	**www.mastercard.com**

Currency converters

Many of the general holiday websites include currency converters, but here are a couple of other addresses for your bookmarks list:

Yahoo!	**http://quote.yahoo.com/m3?u**
Universal Currency Converter	**www.xe.com/ucc**

Chapter 10

Money Online

Introduction

Financial services are ideally suited to the web. After all, most financial products are actually just figures on a screen or page these days. With the rise of credit and debit cards and the ability to transfer money electronically, cash is playing a smaller and smaller part in our lives. And once financial products are reduced to a digital format they become far easier to distribute. Instead of sending cumbersome application forms and statements by post – a slow and inefficient process – product providers can send them across the internet in a few seconds.

There are many advantages to managing your money online. First and foremost, it saves time and hassle. If you're shopping around for a new mortgage, credit card, or personal loan, you would normally have to spend hours on the phone or in the high street picking up leaflets in banks or building society branches. Then you would have the arduous task of trying to compare products, with all their confusing bells and whistles, looking for the best one.

The web gets rid of most of that legwork.

And there are increasing numbers of websites that do most of the research for you, compiling databases of financial products and making it easy to compare them and sort them according to any number of criteria you choose. This ability to sort and sift large volumes of data is something the web is extremely good at.

The web also helps you to keep bang up-to-date with your finances. With internet banking you can get an up-to-date balance whenever you like, and look through all your latest transactions.

This ability to keep up-to-date is a major advantage for investors. You can look up the very latest share prices and stock market news online, and keep pace in a fast-moving environment. You can get valuations of your portfolio whenever you want and buy and sell instantaneously at the click of a mouse.

Buying financial products online can also save you money. Many financial product providers find it cheaper to distribute their products online, direct to the customer. It cuts out the middleman – tied agents and independent financial advisers, for example – and they can pass on some of those savings to you. Online banks that have no branches to maintain can offer higher-than-average interest rates on savings, for example. Credit card providers can offer lower annual percentage rates (APRs) for internet-only cards; insurance companies can offer discounts on policies bought over the web; and independent financial advisers can reimburse their usual commission on unit trust products because of the money they save by doing business online.

As there are many different types of financial website, here's a checklist of questions to ask yourself when you're browsing:

● Is it simply an information provider or is it trying to sell me products?

- If it's just an information provider, how much of the market does it really cover?

- Is it a single company offering only its own products, or an intermediary (broker) offering a range of products?

- Are the products offered by an intermediary unique to it or could you get the same direct from a product provider?

- Are you getting general advice or individual advice based on a detailed understanding of your particular financial circumstances?

Online banking

Almost all banks and building societies now offer online accounts of some sort. The internet-only banks, such as Smile and Cahoot, have given the high-street banks a run for their money with much higher interest rates on current and savings accounts. Switching account providers is becoming easier, stimulating competition to our benefit. We're the bank managers now.

The main advantage of banking online is that you get access to your account information whenever you want. You're no longer restricted to bank opening hours. You can get an up-to-date account balance and review all your most recent transactions – up to six months' worth in some cases. And the visual format is much more helpful than the telephone for taking in large amounts of information. Several banks also allow you to download statements into personal finance management packages. Such ease of access means you stay in control of your finances because you know where you are at all times. Banks are increasingly providing online statements for credit cards as well.

You can usually pay bills online – all you need are the payees' account details. You can set up a list of payees to save having to type in the details every time you need to pay a bill. You just select a payee from the list and enter the amount to be paid. And the great thing is that you can normally specify the date that you want the bill to be paid, sometimes many months in advance. No more missed credit card payments or angry letters from the gas man. It saves time, effort and postage.

If you make regular payments from your bank account you can set up standing orders and then view, amend or cancel them online. Currently, only a few banks let you set them up online, but this is likely to change as the range of internet banking services widens. Most services will also let you transfer funds electronically between accounts, including accounts held at other banks. This is very useful given that many people have more than one bank account.

You can usually communicate with your bank by e-mail, to order a new cheque book, for example – although it has to be said that not many banks have a good reputation for prompt replies.

The only thing we can't do yet is withdraw cash from our PCs and mobile phones. But even that could change over the next few years with the introduction of smartcards – plastic cards containing a computer chip. Before too long we may be able to slot our smartcards into our PCs and download electronic cash from our bank accounts on to the cards. We could then use them to make small purchases over the internet or in shops that have smartcard readers.

Although banking online does offer a number of advantages, convenience being the main one, it has to be said that telephone banking can do much the same job. And several banks are incorporating mobile phone banking into their fleet of services. So it's not a question of one medium superseding another but of a range of options giving customers the power to bank 'any time, anywhere'.

So how do I choose an internet bank?

First of all ask yourself what you want from your bank. Are you simply looking for a high-interest home for your savings, or do you want to carry out a whole range of banking activities as quickly and painlessly as possible? Switching bank accounts can be a hassle – all those direct debits and standing orders to cancel and set up again. Make sure that

the bank you choose offers a good range of services and is one that you feel comfortable with. Find out what its security policies are, what steps it takes to keep your details confidential and what it does if the service crashes.

> **TIP**
>
> *Make sure that the bank you choose offers a good range of services and is one that you feel comfortable with. Find out what its security policies are, what steps it takes to keep your details confidential and what it does if the service crashes.*

Test-drive a few before deciding. Many have demonstrations and tours on their websites to help you get a feel for the service. You'll be surprised at how annoying minor design defects can become after you start using a service a lot.

My top ten banks and building societies with internet accounts:

Abbey National	www.abbeynational.co.uk
Cahoot	www.cahoot.com
Citibank	www.citibank.co.uk
Egg	www.egg.com
First Direct	www.firstdirect.com
Halifax	www.halifax.co.uk
Intelligent Finance	www.if.com
Nationwide	www.nationwide.co.uk

| Northern Rock | **www.northernrock.co.uk** |
| Smile | **www.smile.co.uk** |

Investing online

The internet has given first-time ordinary investors many of the same resources professional investors in the City have always had. These days private investors can buy and sell instantaneously, get up-to-the-second portfolio valuations, read stock market and company news, and bury their noses in tons of research freely available online.

Dealing online is generally cheaper than dealing over the phone because there are no expensive human beings involved – just expensive computer systems. And the great thing about computer systems is that they can handle significantly more traffic without the need for a proportionate increase in computing power. Dealing charges have fallen to £10 and below in some cases.

Although buying and selling shares is the most popular investment activity online, you can also invest in Individual Savings Accounts (ISAs), investment funds, futures and options, and foreign currency. Most online brokers are execution-only – that is, they don't offer any advice based on your individual circumstances. They may well include their own views on the general state of the markets and even give some share tips, but such advice is for all their customers and not just you. The theory is that the type of investor who is happy to trade online is usually savvy enough to do his or her own research, too. But some brokers do offer advice, with the extra cost being incorporated into the dealing commission, or charge separately on an *ad hoc* basis. Check out what kind of service the broker offers before you open an account.

So how do I choose an internet stockbroker?

First you've got to decide what kind of investor you are or intend to be. Ask yourself the following questions, then check out the brokers listed below to find the one that best suits your needs:

● Do you want access to a wide choice of investment products, such as funds, bonds and options, or are you happy just dealing in shares?

● Do you want as much research information at your disposal on your broker's site, or are you happy to find it on other websites?

● Is it important to you to have access to live streaming share prices and news?

● Do you want the option to place orders in a variety of ways, including via telephone, interactive digital television or mobile device?

TIP

If you're keen on the stock market, but unsure how to choose companies or funds to invest in, seek independent financial advice or use an online broker who offers advice.

● Do you want access to foreign markets?

● Do you mind if your investments are held electronically in a nominee account on your behalf and you don't receive share certificates?

● How often are you likely to deal? Low dealing costs will be more important to frequent traders.

● Do you want to shelter your investments inside a tax-free Individual Savings Account?

● Are you sure you don't need one-to-one advice?

● What quality of telephone and/or e-mail support does the broker offer?

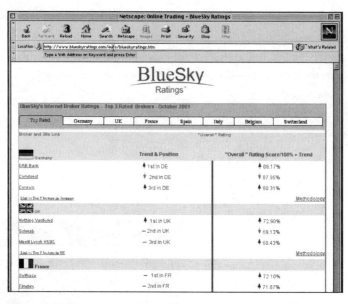

When you're shopping around for a good online stockbroker, ratings and cost comparison services such as those offered by Blue Sky Ratings (www.blueskyratings.com, above) and FT Your Money (http://ftyourmoney.ft.com, below) can help you decide.

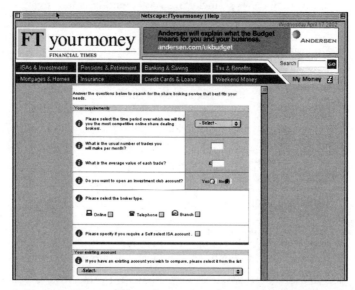

Most of the internet brokers have demos on their sites. Check them out. It's important to get the feel of a service before you sign up. The site may be very sophisticated but poorly designed, or simply not your style. And how much online help do they provide? Some of the information websites mentioned below also provide useful guides to choosing a broker.

Need help shopping around?

At the time of writing there were around 30 online brokers competing for the attentions of approximately 350,000 online investors. That's a lot of shopping around to do. Luckily, there are a few ratings and comparison services around to help you compare brokers on a like-for-like basis. Here are my two favourites:

BlueSky Ratings	**www.blueskyratings.com**
FTYourMoney 'Brokerfinder'	**http://ftyourmoney.ft.com/FTym/brokerfinder**

How does online dealing actually work?

First, you have to open an account. Some brokers allow you to do this online straight away, others require proof of identity documentation, which means it can take up to two weeks to open the account. After that you're usually issued with a user name and password or personal identification number (PIN). This is to prevent anyone going online and buying shares in your name without your authority. Keeping your security details secret is your responsibility. If you lose or forget your password/PIN, most brokers will send it to you by e-mail so long as you can answer another pre-agreed security question.

You normally have to open the account with an initial deposit – some brokers impose a minimum. You can send this by cheque, or make a direct transfer from your bank account, or simply make an online payment using your debit card. Electronic transfer is the easiest. Once you've set up a variable direct debit you can then transfer funds back and forth between your bank and share-dealing accounts very easily.

After that, away you go. Do some research into the companies you're thinking of investing in, using the broker's own research tools and external ones as necessary. When you're ready to trade, you normally go through to the trading section, enter the stock market code of the company you want to buy or sell (there's usually a 'look-up' facility if you don't know it) and then enter the number of shares or the amount you want to invest.

The best brokers will then give you a live price quote that you can either accept or reject. If you like the price, press enter. Most brokers also give you the opportunity to place a 'limit order' where you can specify the price you want to deal at. Normally this is on a 'fill or kill' basis, which means that the deal is cancelled immediately if it can't be completed at the price you want. Some brokers will keep limit orders open until the end of the trading day. This facility also means you can place orders out of market hours – at the weekend, say.

When you've entered your order, you're then normally given a last chance to review it and make sure you haven't made a mistake. Check over the details carefully – there's no going back after this point. If you're happy, press the submit button. Your order is then processed instantaneously (unless there is some reason why it has to be completed manually by the broker – if it is outside normal market size, for example). You're then quoted a unique order number to prove that the transaction was made and executed and sent an electronic contract note recording the terms on which the deal was made. It's a good idea to print these off.

Your orders are scrambled using 128-bit encryption so it's virtually impossible for anyone to intercept confidential information as it is sent across the web. Brokers also have sophisticated 'firewall' security protecting their computer systems from unauthorised infiltration.

My top twenty online brokers:

American Express Sharepeople	www.sharepeople.com
Barclays Stockbrokers	www.barclays-stockbrokers.co.uk
Charles Schwab Europe	www.schwab-europe.com
Comdirect	www.comdirect.co.uk
Deal4Free	www.deal4free.com
DLJ Direct	www.dljdirect.co.uk
e-Cortal	www.e-cortal.com
E*Trade	www.etrade.co.uk
FasTrade	https://www.fastrade.co.uk
Fimatex	www.fimatex.co.uk
Halifax Sharedealing	www.sharexpress.co.uk
Merrill Lynch HSBC	www.mlhsbc.co.uk
IDealing	www.idealing.co.uk
IMIWeb	www.imiweb.com
James Brearley & Sons	www.jbrearley.co.uk
Killik & Co	www.killik.co.uk
myBROKER	www.mybroker.com
Nothing Ventured	www.nothing-ventured.com
Stocktrade	www.stocktrade.co.uk
TD Waterhouse	www.tdwaterhouse.co.uk

Information is power

Although your online broker should offer research resources on its own site, there are plenty of other independent sites to help you with stock selection and investment strategy. Here are my favourites:

WARNING

Sharedealing on the net is very fast and easy to do. It can also become addictive if you're not careful. So make sure you know what you're doing before you speculate away your life savings. You shouldn't invest more than you can afford to lose. Investments can go down as well as up ... etc... etc...

ADVFN (Advanced Financial Network)	www.advfn.com
Ample Interactive Investor	www.iii.co.uk
Citywire	www.citywire.co.uk
FT Investor	www.ftinvestor.com
FTYourMoney	www.ftyourmoney.com
Hemmington Scott	www.hemscott.net
Investors Chronicle	www.investorschronicle.co.uk
London Stock Exchange	www.londonstockexchange.com
Motley Fool UK	www.fool.co.uk
MX Moneyextra	www.moneyextra.com
ShareCast	www.sharecast.com
Teletext	www.teletext.co.uk
This Is Money	www.thisismoney.com
TrustNet	www.trustnet.com
Yahoo! Finance	http://uk.finance.yahoo.com

Investment funds online

The cheapest, most convenient way to buy investment funds is through a fund supermarket. These are services that let you mix and match funds from different fund managers yet keep them all within one tax-free Individual Savings Account (ISA). This means you receive just one consolidated statement, rather than lots of bits of paper arriving at different times. And if you set up a self-select ISA through a stockbroker you can also include shares, bonds and other investments.

Another advantage of buying funds through a supermarket is that the initial charges are usually much lower than you would pay buying direct from the fund manager. For example, you could expect to pay an initial charge of around 5% buying direct. Through a supermarket the initial charge might be 1.5% or less, depending on the type of fund.

Also, if you want to alter the balance of your portfolio as your investment objectives change, switching funds within a supermarket ISA is much quicker and cheaper than the conventional method. Normally you would have to write off to your fund manager requesting a withdrawal then apply to the new fund manager once you'd received your cheque. This is a long-winded process that can take weeks.

Harnessing the power of the internet makes for a more efficient operation. Investors can buy funds online using a debit card, rather than by cheque. It is fast and safe because the card details are encrypted before they cross the internet. Not even the most skilful hacker in the world could intercept and decode your personal data while it was in transit. And the 'always open' nature of the internet also means you can get up-to-the-minute valuations of your portfolios whenever you want. This puts you more in control of your investments.

But perhaps the most significant advantage of fund supermarkets is the breadth of choice. They offer hundreds of funds from scores of managers. This gives you the freedom to be far more sophisticated in the way you build up your portfolios, spreading risk by choosing funds from different geographical areas or investment sectors. And through the use of online performance measurement tools powered by specialist data crunchers, such as Morningstar, Standard & Poor's Micropal, and Lipper, investors can select funds with the best track records and with the right level of risk to suit their investment styles.

I've listed the best online fund supermarkets below:

AISA Direct	**www.aisa.co.uk**
Ample	**www.ample.com**
Barclays Stockbrokers	**www.barclays-stockbrokers.co.uk**
Best Invest	**www.bestinvest.co.uk**
CharcolOnline	**www.charcolonline.co.uk**
Charles Schwab Europe	**www.schwab-europe.com**
Egg	**www.egg.com**
E*Trade	**www.etrade.co.uk**
Fidelity FundsNetwork	**www.fundsnetwork.co.uk**
Funds Direct	**www.fundsdirect.co.uk**
TD Waterhouse	**www.tdwaterhouse.co.uk**
Torquil Clark	**www.tqonline.co.uk**

Pensions online

Pensions have traditionally been sold by independent financial advisers because most of us need help when it comes to retirement planning. But things are changing. The personal pension mis-selling scandal dented confidence in the market to such an extent that the government has devised a new, simpler and cheaper product, known as the stakeholder pension.

Launched in April 2001, it is designed largely for average and below-average earners. But many pension providers have tailored their products to match the new guidelines. The idea is that when investors buy a stakeholder pension they'll know exactly what they're getting, with no hidden costs to worry about. For example, the annual management cost is limited to 1%. This simplification makes them easier to sell online.

There are a number of useful personal finance websites to visit if you want to find out more about stakeholder pensions and how much you need to contribute to reach a certain level of income in retirement. My favourites are:

This Is Money	**www.thisismoney.com**
Ample Interactive Investor	**www.iii.co.uk**
FTYourMoney	**www.ftyourmoney.com**

When researching pension options online, it is a good idea to find out how much your state pension might be worth at retirement age (currently 65 for men and 60 for women). You can fill in an application form (BR19) on the Department for Work and Pensions website (**www.dss.gov.uk**) (formerly the DSS).

To help you shop around for the best provider, try the following sites:

Charcolonline	**www.charcolonline.co.uk**
Discount Pensions	**www.discountpensions.co.uk**
Pensions Network	**www.pensionsnetwork.com**

For a directory of pensions providers, go to:

| FIND | **www.find.co.uk** |

Mortgages, loans and credit cards

The net is a fantastic research tool for borrowers. Lenders seem to take great delight in making their products as complicated as possible. This is fine if it means we consumers get more choice, but it's a nuisance if it makes it impossible to compare products on a like-for-like basis. There are thousands of products out there, so finding the right one is a daunting task. But this is where the net comes into its own, because it can unravel complicated products very easily by sorting masses of data at the speed of light.

Increasingly, personal finance websites are incorporating sophisticated product databases into their services, enabling you to search for specific types of product while filtering out those that don't meet your specific criteria. For example, you may want to exclude mortgages where you have to take the lender's insurance products with the mortgage, or you may want a credit card that charges no annual fee. You can work out just how much you would save by switching to a new lender.

- Personal finance websites help you shop around, and some give personalised advice, too.

WARNING

Make sure you read the small print when you click for more details on 'best buys'. Often the headline interest rate doesn't tell the whole story. There may be geographical restrictions, for example, or the advertised interest rate may apply only for the first six months.

Here are my favourites:

Ample Interactive Investor	**www.iii.co.uk**
Charcolonline	**www.charcolonline.co.uk**
CreditWeb	**www.creditweb.co.uk**
FIND (financial website directory)	**www.find.co.uk**
FT Your Money	**www.ftyourmoney.com**

Moneyfacts	**www.moneyfacts.co.uk**
Moneynet	**www.moneynet.co.uk**
Moneysupermarket	**www.moneysupermarket.com**
Moneywise Magazine	**www.moneywise.co.uk**
MX Moneyextra	**www.moneyextra.com**
This Is Money	**www.thisismoney.com**

When shopping around, make sure you try several sites that offer product comparisons. They don't all update their databases at the same time, and depending on how they input the data, different 'best buys' can emerge. Also go to some direct lenders (use the FIND directory) for comparison.

Insurance

When you're looking to renew your insurance, whether it's travel, pet, life, motor, home or health, there are several options open to you online. Firstly, have a look at the general personal finance portal websites already mentioned above. They contain a wealth of information, from general guides, to 'best buy' tables and links to insurers. Secondly, you can go to an online broker or insurance 'supermarket' that will help you shop around for the best deal, often for several different types of insurance. And thirdly, because you can't assume that the broker will cover the whole market, you should check out a few insurers direct as well.

For each type of insurance, I've selected my favourite websites, chosen mostly for the degree of functionality they offer, particularly the ability to buy online.

Insurance 'supermarkets' and insurance directories

Coversure	**www.coversure.co.uk**
FIND	**www.find.co.uk**
e-Insurance Directory	**www.e-insurancedirectory.com**
Egg	**www.egg.com**

InsuranceWide   **www.insurancewide.com**
The AA   **www.theaa.com**
The Insurance Centre   **www.theinsurancecentre.co.uk**
Quoteline Direct   **www.quotelinedirect.co.uk**
Rapidinsure   **www.rapidinsure.co.uk**

Life insurance

Direct Life and
  Pension Services   **www.dlps.co.uk**
Online Life Insurance   **www.onlinelifeinsurance.co.uk**
Investment Discounts
  Online   **www.theidol.com**
LifePro   **www.ins-site.co.uk**
Life-Search   **www.life-search.co.uk**
Life Policies Direct   **www.lifepoliciesdirect.co.uk**
Online Life Insurance   **www.onlinelifeinsurance.co.uk**

Car insurance

Admiral Insurance   **www.admiral-insurance.co.uk**
Autobytel   **www.autobytel.co.uk**
Churchill   **www.churchill.com**
Direct Line   **www.direct-line.com**
Eagle Star Direct   **www.eaglestardirect.co.uk**
Elephant   **www.elephant.co.uk**
Morethan   **www.morethan.com**
Norwich Union Direct   **www.norwichuniondirect.co.uk**

Home and travel insurance

Direct Line   **www.direct-line.com**
Eagle Star Direct   **www.eaglestardirect.co.uk**
Endsleigh   **www.endsleigh.co.uk**
Norwich Union Direct   **www.norwichuniondirect.co.uk**
Columbus Direct   **www.columbusdirect.net**
Preferential   **www.preferential.co.uk**
STA Travel   **www.sta-travel.com**
The RAC   **www.rac.co.uk**

| Trailfinders | **www.trailfinders.co.uk** |
| Travel-Insurance Direct | **www.travel-insurance.net** |

Advice online

D espite the rise of excellent personal finance websites, many people still need personalised advice, and the web has done a great deal to enhance the services IFAs can offer.

More and more advisers are using the web to speed up communications with their clients and to automate much of the fact-finding they need to do before recommending specific products.

For example, **Sort** (**www.sort.co.uk**) is a service from an IFA firm that allows customers to fill in an online questionnaire detailing their financial circumstances. They e-mail this off to Sort and receive specific product recommendations in return in the form of reports.

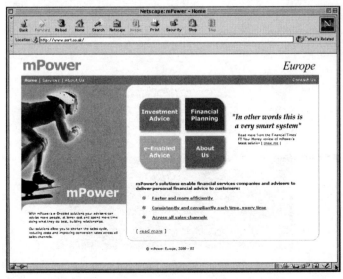

Sort is one of the few companies to offer an online independent financial advice service. More are likely to follow.

The advice goes further than other general infomediary websites because it is individualised. Sometimes IFAs can get better deals for us than we'd get if we went direct to the product provider. The reason for this is that providers often incorporate IFA commissions into the cost of the product. So even if you don't go through an IFA you can still end up paying for it one way or another.

But these days plenty of IFAs will reimburse some or all of the commission they receive from product providers if you transact with them online. Some just offer this anyway as a promotional gimmick. Others will only transact on an execution-only basis, just using their influence with product providers to get you a good deal.

So how do I find an IFA?

At the moment there are no websites that can tell you whether or not specific IFAs are any good, although such a

If you want to find an indepedent financial adviser in your area just type in your postcode at the Society of Financial Advisers website.

ratings service would be useful. But you can start off by
looking at the personal finance websites mentioned above.
Most of them have sections about IFAs and guidance on how
to find a good one.

The Society of Financial Advisers (**www.sofa.org**) also has
an 'Find an Adviser' service on its website. You can search by
postcode, town, or by the IFA's surname. You can also look
specifically for IFAs that specialise in certain areas of advice,
whether tax planning or mortgages. Make sure that the IFA
you choose is qualified to advise on the area of finance
you're interested in. Alternatively, browse the list of IFA
websites on FIND (**www.find.co.uk**), the excellent financial
services directory.

Tax

Again, the personal finance websites listed above usually

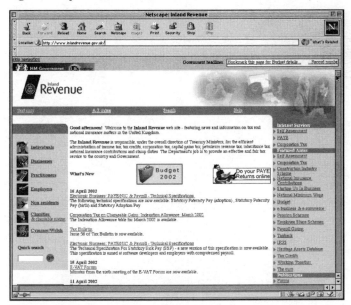

*The Inland Revenue's website is labyrinthine in design, but if you dig around
you can find lots of useful guidance and information on tax matters in a
variety of file formats.*

include general advice and information about tax. But if you fancy filling in your own tax return, here are some useful sites to visit:

Inland Revenue	**www.inlandrevenue.gov.uk**
Digita's Taxcentral	**www.taxcentral.co.uk**
e-Taxchecker	**www.e-taxchecker.co.uk**
Tax Café	**www.taxcafe.co.uk**

And if you want to find an accountant to have an online relationship with, try these firms for starters:

Ascot Drummond	**www.ascotdrummond.co.uk**
SJD Accountancy	**www.sjdaccountancy.com**
Grant Thornton	**www.grant-thornton.co.uk**

Chapter 11

Miscellaneous Services

Introduction

This chapter wraps up some of the miscellaneous other uses you can put the internet to, from downloading music to telephony.

Chat

So-called chat rooms are places where you can engage in almost instantaneous conversations with people by typing in messages and reading their replies. ISPs will often host web chats for their users, inviting guests to take part. AOL and CompuServe have their own chat forums which are safe, controlled environments for you to start in if you're uneasy about the whole concept. Increasingly, companies are using chat rooms as a way of providing customer service online – it's often cheaper to communicate this way than by telephone, though seldom quicker.

Chat rooms are usually organised along subject lines. Go into one room and they'll be talking about one topic, go into another and the subject may be entirely different. Lots of people can be logged on at once, often leading to lively conversations. Eavesdropping on some of these conversations sometimes makes you wonder what people do all day, and who pays the telephone bills! Often it's not the chatters.

The most common chat software program is called **Internet Relay Chat (IRC)**. You can download it from **mIRC** (**www.mirc.com**) if you use a PC, or **IRCLE** (**www.ircle.com**) if you use a Mac. There is lots of help on these sites on how to configure the software and how to find chat servers. The program's own 'Help' file is also useful. You have to give yourself a nickname and also decide whether you want to use your real name and e-mail address at all.

When you enter a chat room your nickname is automatically logged so that everyone else in the room can see you've arrived. Take time to learn how IRC works or else you might end up annoying everyone by entering the wrong commands or earn their general contempt. Again the IRC 'Help' file will tell you most of what you need to know. Generally the system works on the basis of a forward slash signifying that a command follows, such as /JOIN or /EXIT. You can have private conversations within the room, set up your own chat channel and control who you allow in. There are numerous chat conventions and shorthands that can be quite intimidating at first, but you'll soon get to know them if you observe others closely, and they're not compulsory.

Rather than describing how it all works here, just download the software, read all the 'Help' files, go online and read some more FAQs on the IRC sites mentioned above, then try it out.

If you want to find out what's happening in chatland, visit some of these sites:

TalkCity	**www.talkcity.com**
Yack	**www.yack.com**

The Globe	**www.theglobe.com**
Liszt	**www.liszt.com**

Webchat

There are an increasing number of places with chat rooms that you can enter without having to have special software. The rules are generally simpler and it can be less fuss all round. Search engines and portals in particular are adding chat facilities to their range of services.

Private chat

Another popular way to chat online, but more privately, is to use a program like **ICQ** (**www.icq.com**) or **AOL Instant Messenger** (included with the Netscape Navigator browser). When you're online these programs will detect whether any of your friends are online, too, so that you can send a message to them instantly and say hello. You need to set up a 'Buddy List' so that the program can recognise who is your friend and who isn't.

Downloading digital music

The net is transforming the music industry almost overnight thanks to the ease with which we can download music files. We can sample songs before we buy the CD, and buy songs individually, too.

MP3, a digital format for music, has rapidly become the standard for the industry. You can now download MP3 files, store them on your computer or transfer them on to portable digital music players, such as the Diamond Rio. There are no moving parts because it's all digital and you get near CD-quality. For tons of information and links to music sites, just go to **MP3.com** (**www.mp3.com**).

First you need a special software plug-in to listen to music. The latest web browsers have them already built in.

You can download hundreds of free digital music files at mp3.com and sign up for its e-mail newsletter too.

WinAmp (www.winamp.com) is one of the leading media players, along with RealPlayer (www.real.com) and Windows Media Player (www.microsoft.com/windows/windowsmedia/).

For example, Microsoft Internet Explorer includes **Windows Media Player** (www.microsoft.com/windows/windowsmedia/) and Netscape Communicator has **Winamp** (www.winamp.com). These enable you to listen to live radio stations – called **streaming audio** – as well as downloaded music files.

There are alternatives, the most popular being **RealPlayer** (www.real.com), suitable for both PC and Mac users. Apple's own media player is called **QuickTime** (www.apple.com/quicktime).

Digital music gives much more choice and flexibility to consumers. Online music retailers, such as CDNow (www.cdnow.com), are adding digital music downloads to their offering. The rise of CD write-rewrite drives in PCs means we can easily make our own compilation albums in no time.

The one major warning to give about music files is that they are very big. Downloading a three-minute song on a 56kbps modem takes around eight minutes, or 15 to 20 minutes with a 28.8kbps modem. If you want to use a **ripper** program, such as RealJukebox, that can transfer music from your CDs on to your hard drive, you'll need lots of disk space. A typical pop song takes up 2MB to 4MB of space. Just bear this in mind before you decide to put your whole collection on your PC for listening while you work, or before you download entire albums during busy times of the day.

The problem with the digital format is that it is so easy to copy record companies have been up in arms about infringement of copyright. Napster (www.napster.com), a massively-popular digital music file sharing service, has been temporarily shut down while it attempts to resolve these issues with the record companies. Until digital music can be reliably protected from pirates, we're likely to remain in limbo for a while. But one thing is certain: digital distribution of music is here to stay.

Telephoning across the web

You can use your computer to telephone people, too. The difference is that your voice is sent across the telephone network in a different format – the same way that internet data is sent. This format is called Internet Protocol (IP). Net telephony products are sometimes called IP telephony, Voice over the Internet (VOI) or Voice over IP (VOIP).

Net telephony does not yet offer the same quality of telephone service as direct telephone

> **WARNING**
>
> *If you use net telephony, the quality of your connection will only be as good as the state of the net at that time. When the network is busy you may experience delay in hearing the other person, or parts of their words may drop out.*

connections, but things are improving fast. And there are more and more net telephony applications around, such as CoolTalk and Microsoft's NetMeeting, that often come incorporated in the latest versions of web browsers.

There are two categories of IP phone call – those that use the net for the entire length of the journey, and those that go part of the way on the net before joining the normal telephone system at some point. The great thing about pure net calls is that you can phone friends or business partners in far-flung corners of the world very cheaply, because you're still linking up to your ISP at local call rates.

The only drawback, and the reason why it will take some time before net telephony takes off in a big way, is that pure

net calls require both your computer and the computer you're 'ringing' to have special software and equipment to enable them to send and receive voice calls. You need a good sound card in your computer plus a high-quality microphone and speakers. Ideally, a headset – where the earphones and microphone are in one piece – will ensure better quality all round.

The standard PC sound card usually allows only talking or listening (half-duplex), not both simultaneously. This can make for slightly stilted conversations. To replicate the ordinary telephone experience you need a 'full-duplex' card that you then have to install in your computer. Some advanced sound cards already have IP telephony software built in. Once you've got the right hardware you can make calls to other computers through net telephone systems such as **ICQ** (www.icq.com). **VocalTec Internet Telephone** (**www.vocaltec.com**) is another well-known service.

Another difference from conventional telephone calls is that you usually have to schedule the call so that you can both arrange to be online at the same time. If not, you simply won't be able to get through. In the US this isn't so much of a problem because they generally get free local calls allowing them to stay online permanently. In the UK, where free calls have yet to become standard, net telephony takes a little more planning.

Also, the quality of your connection will only be as good as the state of the net at that time. When the network is busy you may experience delay in hearing the other person, or parts of their words may drop out. This is because IP involves your voice being segmented into little packets of data that are then sent individually across the network by the shortest available route. This inevitably means that some packets may get log-jammed on their journey, leading to an imperfect voice quality.

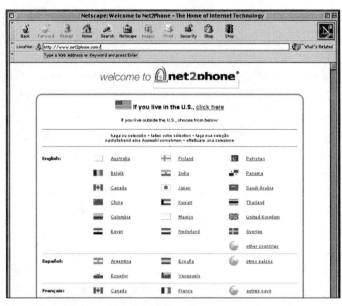

You can cut costs by making telephone calls from your computer to ordinary phones using services such as Net2Phone (www.net2phone.com, above) and iConnectHere (www.deltathree.com, below)

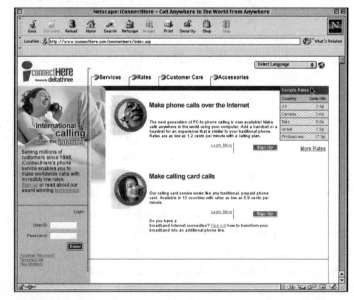

Net-to-phone telephony

Luckily, technology does allow you to make calls from your PC to ordinary phones via so-called 'hop-off' services. These provide gateways between the net and local phone systems in other countries. Such companies do charge for their services, but you're still guaranteed to make savings on international calls.

There are a number of companies that specialise in providing this type of service. Two of the most well-known companies in this area are IDT, which makes **Net2Phone** (**www.net2phone.com**) and **iConnectHere** (**www.deltathree.com**).

If it's just cost you're concerned about, rather than the convenience of using your PC to make calls, you can even use your ordinary phone to ring people across the net using a service such as **Inter-Fone** (**www.inter-fone.com**). Again, the drawback is that both phones need to be connected to the PCs that contain Inter-Fone's own sound cards.

The web goes mobile

You can also access the net from your mobile phone these days, using it to surf specially-created web pages designed for small screens. You can send and receive e-mail and make use of a range of interactive services, from share price alerts to the latest football scores. The initial standard for mobile-friendly web pages was ***Wireless Application Protocol (WAP).***

It has to be said that WAP proved something of a disappointment because the slow data transfer speeds limited the quality of services on offer. The industry is looking towards much faster technologies, such as General Packet Radio Service (GPRS), then Universal Mobile

Telecommunications System (UMTS), before mobile e-commerce really begins to take off. GPRS should have taken over from WAP completely by the end of 2002. For more information on mobile internet services, try the mobile phone operators first:

Vodafone	**www.vodafone.co.uk**
BT Cellnet	**www.btcellnet.co.uk**
T-mobile (formerly One-2-One)	**www.tmobile.co.uk**
Orange	**www.orange.co.uk**
Virgin Mobile	**www.virginmobile.com**

Once the mobile internet really does take off over the next few years, Vodafone, the world's largest mobile operator with over 120 million subscribers, could find itself becoming the UK's largest ISP, putting the likes of Freeserve in the shade. It has already launched **Vodafone Interactive**, which allows customers to specify via the website what information services they want sent to their mobiles.

Virgin Mobile is taking a slightly different approach, equipping its phones with special chip cards inside. These incorporate a mini web browser capable of reading WAP websites. The advantage of this is that you don't have to buy an expensive WAP phone to receive WAP services.

The heartening thing about mobile e-commerce is that for once Europe has stolen a march on the US. European mobile companies have done a much better job than their US counterparts in agreeing technological standards. Mobile phone penetration is also much higher in Europe than in the US. And Nokia, Siemens and Ericsson are now co-operating on a third generation of mobile phone capable of downloading net content more than fifty times faster than current mobiles can manage.

We'll be able to watch live news broadcasts and film trailers on our handsets, shop securely, and access much more visually-rich web pages. Voice-activated services will mitigate the obvious disadvantages of a mobile phone's small keypad and screen, giving us almost complete freedom to roam whilst having an impressive array of communication and transactional resources at our fingertips.

Creating Your Own Web Pages

Introduction

More and more people are taking the opportunity to jump on to the net and make their own contribution to this global community by creating their own web page. If you want to share your wisdom with the rest of the surfing world, advertise your business, or even sell things, then your own website is a must.

Many ISPs now offer free web space to their customers, plus advice on how to use it. There are also plenty of websites dedicated to helping you learn how to set yourself up. For example, **Freewebspace.net** (**www.freewebspace.net**) reviews around 450 free web space providers.

AOL, the world's largest ISP, claims you can get your own web page up and running in 20 minutes flat. Just don't expect design awards to follow. They make it easy for you by using a pre-formatted template. You can include your personal details, enter whatever text you like, add links to other pages and even add sounds. If you have a picture scanner you can even upload a picture of yourself.

Yahoo!'s **Geocities** (**http://geocities.yahoo.com**) offers free web space to members which you can place in a whole range of themed communities. You are also given the tools to create your page. In return, Geocities asks you to include a banner advert for their service on your site and a link back to their home page. Similar free services can be found from **FortuneCity** (www.fortunecity.com) and Lycos's **Tripod** (www.tripod.lycos.com).

Learning HTML

But if you want to get serious about publishing your own website you need to learn a little about HTML – Hypertext Mark-up Language. All web pages are written in HTML. You can create HTML documents using any text editor, such as Notepad if you have a Windows-based PC, or SimpleText if you have a Mac. The latest versions of web browsers contain basic **HTML editors** to help you get started.

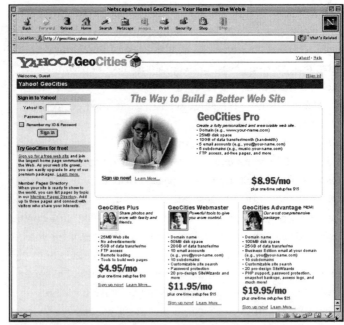

You can build your own website at community sites like Geocities (http://geocities.yahoo.com).

Learning a bit about the fundamentals of HTML is quite a good idea. To denote the various elements in an HTML document, you use *tags*, which are instructions to your computer on how to format the text and images. These comprise a left angle bracket <, a tag name, then a right angle bracket >. For example, <H1> and </H1> would start and end the tag instruction for your main header.

Every HTML document should contain standard HTML tags, such as headings, body text, paragraphs, lists and other elements. First you have to tell the computer that this is an HTML document by writing <html> at the start. Other required elements are <head>, <title>, and <body> tags and their corresponding end tags. To centre a paragraph in your page you would write <P ALIGN=CENTER> at the start of the text and then </P> at the end. You can obviously format your elements any way you like with the relevant tags.

As with learning any new language, it can be daunting at first. But it's just a question of learning the vocabulary. One of the best ways to learn HTML is to see how other people have used it. You can

> **TIP**
>
> *If you want to see how HTML works, choose a simple web page on the net and look at its source file.*

do this by opening up your browser, going to a website you particularly like, and choosing a relatively simple page. In your browser click on 'View', then 'Source' or 'Page Source'. You then see a window with all the HTML commands used to create that page. You may be surprised how few commands it can take to create a relatively complicated-looking page. Then again, if you choose a complicated page – your ISP's home page, for example – the HTML commands can run to several pages if you print them off.

There's no point going into all the ins and outs of HTML in a general guide like this. If you really want to get to grips with the language, you can look at sites on the net that explain it in detail.

What you see is what you get (WYSIWYG)

Website design starts to get complicated when you want to introduce dynamic features such as animated colour graphics, sound, or video. Luckily, there are web authoring tools that enable you to create pages visually rather than writing large swathes of HTML code. These are called WYSIWYG editors – What You See Is What You Get – such as Microsoft FrontPage or Macromedia's Dreamweaver. You can usually find evaluation versions of these packages on free CD-ROMS accompanying computer and internet magazines.

Bear in mind that these packages are designed to meet the needs of professional designers, so you'll need to spend a long time getting to know how they work to get the most out of them. If you simply want a web page as an alternative business card, you don't need such sophisticated tools.

Also, the more you stuff your site with complex graphics and groovy sound files, the more web space you use up. Before too long you may find that you've used up the web space allocated to you by your ISP. The more sophisticated you become with your web page designs, the more likely it is that you will encounter newer versions of HTML, such as DHTML and XML, and other programming and scripting languages such as Java, JavaScript, ActiveX, and CGI. This is seriously complicated stuff and is unlikely to affect the new user, so we don't have to go into it here, thank goodness.

Design tips

Generally speaking, the simpler you keep your web pages, the easier they will be to understand and the faster they will download into people's browsers. And let's face it, unless you've got something pretty compelling to offer, you're going to need every enticement to make people access your site.

Offering a simple, no-fuss site that is quick to load certainly helps.

If you're going to have a website you may as well do it properly. That doesn't necessarily mean opting for all the latest fancy graphics and scripting tools. It means keeping it up to date and trying to fill the site with information that is useful, entertaining or both. It can be very annoying for surfers when they spend time browsing through a site only to discover eventually that the information hasn't been updated since 1996 and is virtually useless. So put the date of the last time you updated your page in a prominent position.

Earning trust

One of the problems the net faces is authenticating and verifying the information and opinions scattered across all these millions of websites. When surfers land on a site purporting to be the world's leading resource on Persian cats, say, how do they know that the author isn't an ignoramus posing as an expert, or worse, just dangerously deranged? The truth is that we don't. So if you're imparting information or opinions to the world, readers of your site are likely to be somewhat sceptical. And who can blame them?

If you want people to trust you and believe you, make an effort to establish your credentials. Tell people about yourself, maybe give a short career résumé, and give a contact address, telephone number, or e-mail. You've got to persuade strangers to your site that you know what you're talking about. Obviously, if you're worried about protecting your privacy, you should be selective in how much personal information you give away, and maybe stick to providing your e-mail address only.

State your sources if you are using research to back up an argument and clarify whether your views are mere personal opinion. Also bear in mind that although the web is often compared to the Wild West without the bullets, you are still governed by the same libel laws as other published material. If you use your web page as a platform to accuse your enemies of unspeakable practices you may well end up before the beak.

Web authoring tools

Macromedia's DreamWeaver	www.dreamweaver.com
Microsoft's FrontPage	www.microsoft.com/frontpage
NetObjects' Fusion	www.netobjects.com
Adobe GoLive	www.adobe.com/golive

Web page design advice

Web Developer	www.webdeveloper.com
eFuse	www.efuse.com
Webmonkey	www.webmonkey.com
Builder.com	www.builder.com
Developer.com	www.developer.com
Web Site Garage	www.websitegarage.com
Davesite	www.davesite.com/webstation
University of Leicester	www.mcs.le.ac.uk/html/BasicHTML.html

Editing web graphics

Adobe PhotoShop	www.adobe.com/photoshop
Macromedia Fireworks	http://www.macromedia.com/software/fireworks/
Hemera Technologies NetGraphics Studio	www.hemera.com

Where should I keep my website?

When you've designed your website, you don't have to keep it on your ISP's server. There are plenty of **web hosting services** around. These are companies that look after your website for you, store your web pages, and ensure that your site is available to the public 24 hours a day, seven days a

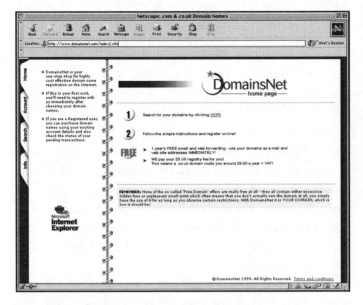

Register your domain name with a service such as DomainsNet (www.domainsnet.com).

week. Should you want to turn your website into a commercial venture, a web hosting service can usually handle online payments, too.

If you want your website to have a distinctive name, it's essential that you register the domain name. That's the website name plus the abbreviation after the dot. You can do this via a number of domain name registration companies, such as **DomainsNet** (**www.domainsnet.com**) or **Nicnames** (**www.nicnames.co.uk**). It usually costs between £40 and £100, depending on the level of other services they offer. It will often take a long time entering your proposed domain names until you find one that hasn't been taken. Most of the obvious ones were snapped up a long time ago. This is perhaps why so many web services have silly names.

Owning your own domain name gives you more freedom over your e-mail address, too. You can have 'anyname@your-domain-name.co.uk' and the company will forward e-mails sent to this address to your existing e-mail address.

A web hosting service will usually handle the domain name registration part for you, as well as e-mail and URL forwarding. URL forwarding means that surfers typing in your web address, based on your new domain name, will first go to the hosting company's servers before being bounced on to wherever you've decided to keep your website.

Most companies will offer you at least 20MB of space – enough for a small-scale website. But if you're planning something major, you may need to have an entire computer dedicated to handling your site. This can cost up to £10,000 a year, so make sure yours is a serious commercial venture before you opt for this!

It is tempting to stick with the free web space offered by your ISP, and in most cases this will be good enough for people just wanting to have a bit of fun. But if you are more serious about establishing a web presence, reliance on your ISP can backfire in the long-term. For example, **Freeserve** (**www.freeserve.com**) doesn't allow you to use your own domain name on its servers – you have to accept whatever name it gives you. If you're set on having your own name, you have to move your site somewhere else, which can be irksome to say the least.

> ### TIP
>
> *Most ISPs will offer you at least 20MB of space, which should be plenty for a small-scale website.*

Another point to bear in mind is that not all ISPs will allow you to conduct commercial activities on websites that they host. If you plan to move into business, check first with your ISP and any proposed hosting service that they do allow this. Sometimes ISPs will not allow you to use the software necessary to run your own commercial website – product catalogues, for example, or application forms, for fear that

Reviewing the whole world of free web space (www.freewebspace.net).

you'll crash their servers and put all their members' noses out of joint.

Free web hosting services, such as those listed by **FreeWebSpace (www.freewebspace.net)** may seem tempting, but just be aware of the potential drawbacks. For example, some service providers can be quite inflexible about what you can and can't do with your site.

As with most things in life, you generally get what you pay for. The more you cough up, the more comprehensive will be the list of services on offer, the web space provided, and the freedom to run things the way you want. For around £200 a year you can get your own domain name, plus shared space on a web hosting company's server. But there may be limitations on the amount of *traffic* your site can receive. Traffic is the term used for the flow of visits websites receive from browsing surfers.

It is possible to host your site in the US. There is greater competition over there so prices are generally lower. But your pages may download more slowly because of the greater distance they have to cover.

If you're shopping around for a web hosting service, go to **www.findahost.com** and **www.tophosts.com** for reviews and comparisons. Some internet magazines also publish the result of monthly tests on web hosting companies.

Here's a checklist of what the perfect web hosting service should offer:

● technical support 24 hours a day, seven days a week

● website design advice

● a chance to visit their premises and check the security of the site

● back-ups in case of server corruption or theft

● business references and favourable reviews

● online shopping service

● fast connection times

● the facility to handle more sophisticated pages that may include video and audio

● no restrictions on the amount of traffic your site can receive

● low charges if you decide to move your site to another host in future

How will people know about my website?

It is surprisingly common for companies who should know better to set up websites and then expect a flood of visitors as soon as they're up and running. If only it were that simple. The internet is a very big place and the chances of anyone

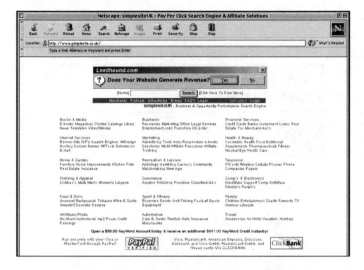

By including links to commercial companies you might be able to make money through your website.

landing on your site at random are miniscule. Don't forget, there are over eight billion web pages out there!

One way to publicise your website is to get other websites to publish a link to yours. You can usually do this for free if you come to a reciprocal arrangement – I'll link to yours if you link to mine. A fancy link including graphics is called a **banner ad** and services such as Microsoft's **bCentral** (**www.bcentral.com**) offer a range of useful promotional ideas for businesses, including affiliate marketing. If someone comes to your site and clicks on one of these commercial links on your pages – known as a **click through** – you get a small percentage of any sale that results. **SimpleSite** (**www.simplesite.co.uk**) has a list of all the affiliate schemes you could sign up to.

Big companies pay millions of pounds to advertise their sites on popular portal sites and search engines because they know millions of people are going to visit those sites and see their ads. It's the same as conventional newspaper, magazine

Get a handle on how search engines prioritise website addresses at Search Engine Watch (www.searchenginewatch.com).

and television advertising. The more traffic you can direct to your site, the more attractive it will appear to potential advertisers and the more money you'll make.

Presuming you're not in the big league yet – and if you are you shouldn't really need to read this guide! – another common way to advertise your site is to submit details of your URL to all the search engines and directories. It's free. The problem is that they all have different ways of indexing sites. Some will just pick out key words on your site, others will index it in full, others will accept summaries of what your site contains. You should spend some time investigating what methods they use – **Search Engine Watch** (**www.searchenginewatch.com**) is a useful site to look at.

If you haven't the time or the inclination to do all this yourself, you can leave it to other companies to submit your website and/or promote it for you (see list on *page 236*).

If you're lucky, your site may be picked up by the more thorough search engines anyway, even if you do nothing. Their 'spiders' or 'bots' are constantly scouring the entire web for new pages to add to their databases.

Getting your site to come up when people search on related words is a black art – it mystifies lots of companies. Mostly it involves using meta tags – key words that help to identify the main subjects covered by your site. These are the words that search engines will focus on when trying to sort out searches for relevance. Pornography sites in particular have shamefully picked up on this ruse and often include innocuous words among their meta tags to try to lure unsuspecting people into their lairs (*see Safety, Security and Your Rights, page 248* for more on how to screen out adult content on the web). You often hear at dinner parties how a quite innocent search threw up some far-from-innocent material.

You could also try advertising your website in newsgroups and mailing lists. Obviously it makes sense to target your ads at groups with similar interests. Then there's the trusty paper-based advertising methods of old, such as letter-heads, business cards, printed T-shirts and other merchandise. Many 'dot com' companies still believe such offline advertising to be the most effective.

Some well-known web hosting services

Corpex	www.corpex.com
WebFusion	www.webfusion.co.uk
Global Internet	www.global.net.uk
EasySpace	www.easyspace.co.uk
Verio	www.verio.co.uk

Submitting your website

Addme!	www.addme.com
Broadcaster	www.broadcaster.co.uk

| Submit It | www.submit-it.com |
| Exploit | www.exploit.com |

Promotion and ranking services

| Web Promote | www.webpromote.com |
| Web Position Agent | www.webposition.com |

Chapter 13

Safety, Security and your Rights

Introduction

When we talk about security on the net, there are
several issues involved. Firstly, there is the issue of
privacy – preventing our e-mail from being read by others,
and our personal details abused by websites. Then there's the
problem of how to protect our children from exposure to
unsuitable web content.

Thirdly, there's the issue of secure online shopping –
using our credit and debit cards online safely without fear of
those details being stolen. Fourthly, there's a big issue
surrounding authenticity – websites and surfers proving that
they are who they say they are and that they will deliver
what they promise to deliver. And lastly, there are those
dreaded viruses to worry about – malicious or unintentionally
damaging programs – threatening to invade our hard drives
and reduce them to so much digital rubble.

These are all serious issues. But they are being tackled
and largely overcome by technology and public awareness.
Yet the public perception is that the net is besieged by
millions of fiendishly clever computer hackers breaking into
computers everywhere, stealing our money, reading our

e-mail, corrupting our hard drives, and compromising the defence of our nations on a daily basis. This just isn't true.

Yes, there have been a number of high-profile cases of credit card numbers being stolen from online retailer databases and published on the web. Anyone using those numbers can in theory go on spending sprees until the cards are cancelled. And yes, hackers do consider it a matter of professional pride to try to crack the best security systems that software companies can throw at them. But their activities are, in the main, not malicious. In fact, many argue that they are acting in the public interest by pointing out these security flaws. After all, software companies make great claims about the impenetrability of their security software when they flog it to companies. So shouldn't those businesses be made aware if they are being sold a pup?

It's a moot point, and there's no getting away from the fact that breaking into other people's computer systems is still against the law. But the net result – if you'll pardon the pun – is that these software companies are forced to work harder to improve their products, and we, the public, benefit in the long run because we have a safer environment in which to surf.

It seems that not a day goes by without yet another rumour of a super-virus sweeping the net, each more potentially damaging than the last. Many of these rumours turn out to be hoaxes. Again, I don't want to belittle the security issue. Viruses do exist and they can cause considerable damage. But a good anti-virus software package, regularly updated, can protect you adequately. They're not that expensive, and are easy to download and operate.

> **TIPS**
>
> *Many virus warnings are hoaxes. For a comprehensive list of myths, hoaxes and urban legends have a look at www.vmyths.com.*

The problem is that the media in general like nothing more than a good net scare story. The net is still new so it's exciting to write about, yet many are still largely ignorant about it. And as we generally fear what we don't know, it becomes a vicious circle of misinformation leading to a disproportionate level of suspicion and concern.

The bottom line is that there are ways to deal with these security issues and protect yourself while you're online with a combination of software and common sense. Nowadays we don't think twice about driving with a seat-belt on – it's a necessary precautionary measure. We generally believe that the benefits of driving outweigh the dangers. There should be no difference surfing the net. Bear in mind also that it is in software companies' interests to overhype security fears to help them sell more of their security software!

Bluffer's guide to encryption

Encryption is a way of encoding information so that it can be transferred across an open network, such as the net, without anyone being able to understand what the message is. Only the intended recipient has the 'key' to unlock the code. The data is jumbled up according to a mathematical formula or algorithm and the way these rules are implemented depends on a variable cryptographic key – a string of ones and noughts, basically. A 40-bit key has 40 ones and noughts and a 128-bit key has ... well, you get the picture.

To find the key you have to guess the precise arrangement of ones and noughts. This is well-nigh impossible for us mere mortals but easier for extremely powerful computers which can crunch billions of numbers per second. Codes have been cracked, but this shouldn't worry us unduly, because it took a massive amount of computing power to do it.

A code-cracking machine designed by the Electronic Frontier Foundation in the US searched more than 88 billion keys every second for 56 hours before finding the right 56-bit key to decrypt an encoded message. But to crack a code that used 128-bit encryption you would need computing power more than 1,000,000,000,000 times greater than that used to decrypt a 40-bit message. This is currently impossible and likely to remain so for the foreseeable future.

The key to successful cryptography is not discovering a completely fool-proof code, but making it so difficult that it's not worth anyone's while to try to decode it. As long as the value of the prize is lower than the cost of winning it, encryption should deter criminals. A criminal who can easily get your credit card number from a carbon paper receipt in a shop or restaurant is hardly going to bother linking up 250 computers on the off-chance that he might intercept your number as it whizzes through cyberspace.

There are two main types of encryption: symmetric (secret key) and asymmetric (public key). Symmetric means that the same key is used to encrypt and decrypt the message, and asymmetric means one key is used to encrypt and another to decrypt. Everyone has two keys, a public and a private one. When you want to send an encrypted message you use the recipient's public key, which sits on your computer in the form of a digital certificate. The recipient decodes the message using their private key. It is actually a lot more complicated than that, but you don't really need to know all the gory details.

The digital certificates can also establish the authenticity of the person sending the message and the fact that the message hasn't been tampered with in transit. They are managed and distributed by 'trusted third parties', such as VeriSign and GlobalSign.

Encryption is controversial because the stronger you make it, the more governments think it will help criminals to conceal their activities from law enforcement agencies. The US government does now allow the export of 128-bit encryption products. Before this we had to make do with 40-bit or 56-bit encryption for online transactions.

Privacy

Anonymous e-mail

It is possible for spammers to glean your e-mail address from web pages, chat rooms, directories and Usenet discussion groups using special software. Some programs making use of the JavaScript language can even obtain your e-mail address when you click on icons in web pages. And you don't have much control over what happens to your sent mail when it arrives at its destination. If it is archived, your address is potentially open to hacking over a long period of time.

One way to stop people getting hold of your address is not to give your address out at all. But often this isn't practical, as lots of sites ask you to register with them first before you can use their services, and this involves giving your name and e-mail address. Another way is to use a webmail account, using an address with a made-up user name (*see E-mail, page 109*). Giving a false address is another option, but not much good if you want the website to send you a regular newsletter, for example. You should assume that all mail you send and receive at work is accessible by your employers, so be careful what you say.

When accessing Usenet discussion groups there may be times when you want to remain anonymous yet take part in the discussions. There are a number of services that will help you do this. Anonymous remailers, as they're sometimes known, strip all the headers from your message. Headers are all those lines of information at the top of an e-mail that list who sent the message and by what route it arrived with you. Once you've stripped away all these the person receiving the message would not be able to tell who sent the message nor be able to respond. But obviously this kind of e-mail has to be used responsibly and is open to abuse by cyber-stalkers and other online trouble-makers.

Here are a few services to try out:

PrivacyX   **www.privacyx.com**
Anonymizer   **www.anonymizer.com**
Zed-Zed dot Net   **www.zedz.net**
Anonymous.to   **http://anonymous.to**
Junkbusters   **www.junkbusters.com**

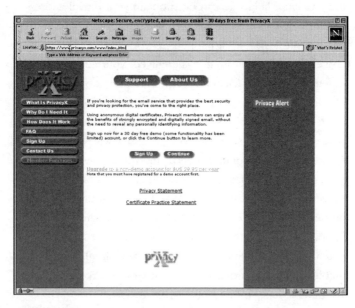

You can protect your privacy when e-mailing by using a service such as Privacy X (www.privacyx.com).

The content of spam e-mails is covered by the British Codes of Advertising and Sales Promotion, the Control of Misleading Advertisements Regulations 1988, and the Trade Descriptions Act 1968. Complain to the relevant body if the claims being made in such e-mails clearly contradict any of these codes and laws.

The Direct Marketing Association also runs a useful e-mail preference service. You can register your e-mail address on the site if you don't wish to receive unsolicited e-mails from any of its members. As most direct marketing companies are members of the DMA, this is a pretty comprehensive service.

Once you've registered on the site all DMA members have to delete your address from their mail lists. The EU's Distance Selling Directive will also require that e-mails for distance selling purposes should only be used when there is no clear objection from the consumer. This means that you will have the chance to choose not to receive unsolicited e-mails and have your choice respected.

If spam continues to be a problem, you may also be able to get help from the Data Protection Registrar, who polices the use of personal data held on computers. The only snag is that the Registrar's powers are limited to the UK, so foreign-sourced e-mails are out of bounds.

Digitally signing and encrypting e-mail

E-mail can be likened to a postcard in that people can potentially intercept and read it while it's en route to its destination. Your ISP could potentially read it while it sits on its servers. For most of us, this wouldn't be a problem even if it did happen, which is unlikely. Not many of us have state secrets to tell, after all.

But there are moves to make the digital signature and encryption of e-mail more widespread. Digital signatures are an attempt to prove that the e-mail really did come from you and no-one tampered with it on the way. Encryption is a way of jumbling up digital data so that it cannot be read by anyone who does not have the key to unscramble the message (*see the Bluffer's guide to Encryption on page 239*).

The latest versions of web browsers have encryption facilities already built in. Digital signing and encryption rely on you downloading a digital certificate from a 'trusted third party' – a company such as VeriSign, British Telecom, Thawte and GlobalSign – that specialises in security products. In the latest version of Outlook you can be taken directly to a Microsoft page that gives links to various certificate providers. Click on 'Tools', 'Options', 'Security', then 'Get a digital ID'. VeriSign (**www.verisign.com**) is Microsoft's preferred certificate supplier and you can try out a certificate for a free trial period.

For information on security options in Messenger, click on 'Communicator', 'Tools', 'Security info', then 'Yours' under the 'Certificates' header. Click on 'Get a certificate' and you'll connect to Netscape's site where you'll find that VeriSign is its preferred partner, too.

Here are the addresses for other certificate distributors:

GlobalSign	**www.globalsign.com**
ChamberSign	**www.chambersign.co.uk**
Thawte	**www.thawte.com**
British Telecom Ignite	**www.ignite.com**

(in association with VeriSign)

Once you've downloaded your certificate you can then choose to sign your messages automatically or do so on an ad hoc basis. But for the digital signature to be any use, your recipients need to install your certificate on their computers. They can install it next to your entry in the address book. Their mailer programs must be able to support this level of security though.

The problem is that digitally signing an e-mail doesn't necessarily prove it was sent by you. It really just proves that the message originated from your *computer*. Someone else who had access to the computer and who knew your e-mail password could send messages purporting to come from you. This is made all the more feasible by the fact that in your dial-up software you can opt to have your computer remember your password, so that's it's already there in the box when you log on.

So if you really want to protect yourself you should also turn off the 'Save password' option. This is simple to do. When you log on a dial-up box normally appears on your screen as it goes through the process of trying to connect, verify password, and so on. In the latest versions of dial-up software, bundled in with your operating system, there is a box you can tick if you want the system to remember your password. Make sure this box is left unticked. After that, just make sure that you keep your password to yourself.

To encrypt your messages, you need to install recipients' certificates on your system as well so that each of you can encrypt and decrypt each other's messages. This is all a bit of a rigmarole and you may well conclude that it's not really worth it, given the largely

> **TIP**
>
> *To stop anyone sending a message from your computer in your name, make sure you have the 'save password' option switched off – and don't go giving out your password!*

innocuous nature of your e-mail. It is really much more of a burning issue for businesses at the moment, who could well be sending messages containing commercially sensitive information.

In the private sphere, digital signing and encryption of e-mail is likely to remain a minority sport among technology enthusiasts, at least until certificates become much more widely spread.

Anonymous surfing

When you browse the net, you leave a trail behind you that can be monitored by websites for marketing purposes. Website operators can sometimes find out the IP address of the machine you used to access their site, the type of computer and browser you used, and the last page you were at before you went to their site. They may also be able to determine your e-mail address and real name.

Ask your ISP if it supports dynamic IP, which means you are assigned a different IP address every time you log on. This makes it far harder for websites to prove that you are the same person returning to their site. If you stay online for a very long time though, it still may be possible for the site to identify you.

TIP

If you want more control over your cookies, allowing those from sites you trust and filtering out the ones you don't, there are several programs around that can help. ZDNet has a lot of shareware versions listed on its site at www.zdnet.co.uk/software, including Cookie Pal, Cookie Monster, Cookie Clutter and Anti-Cookie Suite.

The most common way for websites to log your visit is to send little files called **cookies** to your computer's hard drive when you're online. A cookie is a text file that records your preferences when you use a particular site. Cookies allow the server to store its own identity file on your computer and also for the website to recognise you when you return. This saves you having to log in each time and enables the website to target adverts and services at you according to your preferences.

The threat from cookies has been overstated – they can be quite useful and most of them don't collect personal information about you, such as your name, phone number or e-mail address. Some web pages won't even load properly unless you set your browser to accept them. But they will record how many times you've been to a site and what you did when you were there.

Cookies are stored in a subdirectory on your hard drive. To have a look at them, go to the 'Cookies' folder in the 'Windows' directory, or the 'Users' folder in the 'Netscape' folder. You can tell your browser how to handle cookies, from accepting them all, to rejecting them all. In Explorer, choose 'Tools', 'Internet Options', 'Security', then the 'Internet zone'. Click on 'Custom level' then scroll down to the cookies section and tick the relevant boxes. In Navigator, click on 'Edit', 'Preferences', 'Advanced' and make your choice.

If you want to know more about privacy issues in general have a look at the site of the World Wide Web Consortium, known as W3C for short (**www.w3.org**). It's a coalition of leading net companies recognised to be the arbiter of standards on the net. It is in the process of developing a set of privacy standards whereby the net user will be told what the website's privacy policy is before any kind of transaction takes place. It's called the Platform for Privacy Preferences, or P3P for short. Other informative sites include the Electronic Privacy Information Centre (**http://epic.org**) and Privacy International (**www.privacy.org/pi**).

Anti-virus software

Every surfer should have anti-virus software installed. It's not difficult to do and is essential to protect your computer against invader programs causing a nuisance on your system. Most virus warnings are hoaxes and the threat from viruses is overhyped, but files do become corrupted from time to time even without the hacker's influence. You should be particularly wary of e-mail attachments, especially if they are word processing or spreadsheet documents. The latest anti-virus packages will monitor your e-mail for you and spot attachments containing viruses. They will normally be able to squish or 'clean' the file immediately. ISPs often perform systematic anti-virus checks on your e-mail before you even get it. All in all, you shouldn't get too concerned.

There are three main packages to choose from:

Dr. Solomon's Home Guard **www.drsolomon.com**
McAfee VirusScan　　　　　**www.mcafee-at-home.com**
Norton AntiVirus　　　　　　**www.symantec.com**

When you buy a new computer, an anti-virus package will sometimes be included with the software bundle you get. Bear in mind that the program may have been sitting on the hard drive for several months after manufacture and will more than likely be out of date. Visit the software company's website and download the latest file containing all the known viruses, known as the signature file or the virus definition file. Your anti-virus package can detect which file version you have and tell you whether you need to download a new version. Once you've paid the £30 or so for the basic package, updates are usually free.

Filtering web content

For many parents, the ease with which unsuitable material can be accessed on the web is frightening. They fear that this box in their homes will corrupt the minds of their children instantly. It is true that pornography and anti-social content is easy to find with a few well-chosen words in a search engine – even with a few innocently-chosen words. And there are some bomb-making nutters and unsavoury characters out there. But hey, the net is all about freedom of speech. Freedom is its lifeblood. As with most concerns about the net, there are sensible steps you can take to reduce the risk, and technology is once more coming to our aid.

Firstly, it is possible to set passwords for your computer so that no-one can get access without you being there. Secondly, you could supervise all online activity and surf the web with your children. Thirdly, both leading web browsers incorporate security features that allow you to filter web content. Using the standard Platform for Internet Content Selection (PICS), they allow you to select the level of content you are prepared to accept in four categories of language, sex, nudity and violence.

In Internet Explorer go to 'Tools', 'Internet Options', then click the 'Security' tab. In Navigator select 'NetWatch' under the 'Help' menu. One problem with these PICS settings is that they can be extremely sensitive. Set them to a moderate security level and you often find that you cannot access the most harmless-seeming of pages. Every time you try to access such a 'banned' page, you'll be told you're not authorised to do so without entering the password. This can become extremely tiresome after just a few seconds, so some experimentation is definitely required. I suspect that at this current rather clumsy level most people just disable these ratings after a while. Any system like this will inevitably be subjective. One person's view of offensive is another's idea of a good laugh.

There are stand-alone web filtering packages on the market for around £30 to £40 that can offer a more thorough, less blunt approach. Here is a comprehensive list of the best ones:

Cyber Patrol	www.cyberpatrol.co.uk
The Bair Filtering System	www.thebair.com
Chaperon 2000 (C2K)	www.edu-tec.com
Cyber Sentinel	www.securitysoft.com
CYBERsitter	www.solidoak.com
Cyber Snoop	www.cyber-snoop.com
FamilyConnect 2000	www.cleansurf.com
Net Nanny	www.netnanny.com
PureSight Education	www.puresight.net
RM SafetyNet Plus	www.rm.com/safetynet
SafeKids.Com	www.safekids.com
SafeSurf	www.safesurf.com
SurfControl	www.surfcontrol.com
We-Blocker	www.we-blocker.com
X-STOP	www.xstop.com

Choosing the best filtering package

With so many filtering options around, how do you pick the best? This depends largely on how you and your family use the internet, the age of your children, and how liberal you are about the language, images and other content they are allowed to see. No single solution is necessarily the best for everyone.

Luckily, there are some good reviews around to help you decide. For example the Parents Information Network (www.pin.org.uk), an independent organisation set up to help parents use computers and the internet more effectively, carried out an extensive review of most of the leading packages. Its findings are summarised below:

❶ There is no agreed standard way to solve the problems of monitoring and protection.

❷ There is a huge variation in the rationale behind products and in the methods they offer.

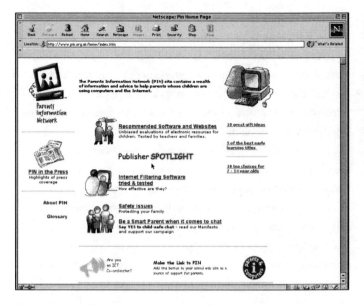

Keep informed about online security and safety issues with the Parents Information Network (www.pin.org.uk).

❸ No single product was found to combine all available filtering features.

❹ There is no agreed quality standard of technical performance or user support.

❺ When tested, most programs did not work as effectively as advertised.

❻ Different kinds of families need different kinds of monitoring and protection and so must search for products that suit their needs.

❼ Products need to be updated regularly to cope with changing patterns of internet use, changing content of websites and new ways to access online resources. None of them provides a permanent solution for parents.

The Consumers' Association magazine **Which?** (**www.which.net**) also carried out a review of a selection of filtering packages in its May 2000 edition. Significantly, not one of the seven packages it tested successfully blocked all of the sites that *Which?* chose in its experiment. This merely adds weight to the view that such packages are only a partial answer to the problem of internet security.

Always bear in mind that even the most sophisticated filtering and monitoring software isn't going to deter the most ingenious and persevering teenager from finding ways around the security measures. And there is always the danger that when something is forbidden it just becomes all the more exciting and a greater challenge. Cod-psychology aside, a combination of software and common sense should guard your children against the worst excesses the net can throw at us.

The 'walled garden' approach

If you're not happy with the level of security offered by web filtering software, you could go one step further and restrict access to a pre-selected list of websites. Once inside this 'walled garden', kids theoretically can't gain access to the World Wide Web. There are several ways these walled gardens can be operated, from CD-ROMs containing all the web pages – so in effect it's just educational software – to tailor-made web browsers that allow access only to the vetted list of sites and no others.

Some internet service providers will carry out the selection themselves, others will allow the parent or teacher to modify the list. In some versions, those in possession of a password can leapfrog the wall and gain unrestricted access. This way, users of all ages can make the most of the internet.

Walled gardens offer several advantages. Firstly, they are very secure. Once inside you can be pretty sure that young children won't be able to gain access to unsuitable material – providing you trust the product provider's choices! This means that internet usage doesn't have to be monitored. Secondly, they are very easy to set up – there are none of the complex adjustments that are usually required with filtering software.

But walled gardens have their limitations, too. They are only as good as the quality of sites selected. They don't actually teach older children how to surf the web responsibly and safely. And once the child has outgrown the level of the pre-selected sites, the walled garden ceases to have any appeal.

Also, a sophisticated child could easily skirt around the walled garden – by opening an alternative web browser, for example, and searching for inappropriate material via a search engine. Increasingly, search engines and directories are incorporating their own safety features, such as password requirements for adult-orientated searches. Others are restricting their web page databases to child-friendly websites. But as with filtering software, even the walled garden approach isn't necessarily 100% safe.

Below are some examples of walled garden services. However, be warned that some of the more commercial services listed will include adverts. Some parents may find such intrusions unpalatable.

Grid Club for Kids (www.gridclub.com)
The first rule of Grid Club is that everyone should talk about Grid Club. It's an out-of-school club designed to be a safe environment where kids aged seven to 11 can interact with each other, play games, and get help with homework and revision. It is a DfEE-funded project, admittedly still in its

infancy, but with great potential. Safety is assured because the clubs the children belong to are hosted within a protected environment at Think.com, created by Oracle, the US computer systems giant. The clubs are run by club leaders who look after the children and monitor all the written communication. Every child who wants to be a member of Grid Club has to obey the club rules.

@kidz (www.atkidz.com)
Another controlled ISP service involving CD-ROM software, @kidz provides controlled access to e-mail and online chat for kids, plus homework help and educational fact files.

AT Kids Browser (www.winshare.com/mkbindex.htm)
A multimedia web browser that provides an education-oriented filtered environment for children to surf the internet.

ChiBrow (www.chibrow.com)
Another dedicated web browser designed for children, which parents can program to define which sites their offspring have access to.

AngliaCampus (www.angliacampus.com)
Content service developed from Anglia Interactive and CampusWorld services.

AOL (www.aol.com)
The world's largest ISP has made great play of its child- and parent-friendly environment. As AOL offers its own browser to members it can offer more control over what children are allowed to see. Its Parental Controls section allows adults to set a security level for each person who uses AOL.

Ask Jeeves for Kids (www.ajkids.com)
A search engine tailored to find child-friendly sites only.

Awesome Library (www.awesomelibrary.org)
Over 18,000 librarian-reviewed resources for kids.

KidsClick (http://sunsite.berkeley.edu/kidsclick!)
More librarian-vetted websites for kids.

Kid's Search Tools (www.rcls.org/ksearch.htm)
A meta-search engine allowing kids to search using several child-friendly search sites.

Yahooligans! (http://yahooligans.com)
Another tailored web directory from the world's largest search portal Yahoo!

Safety in chat rooms

There has been a great deal of justified concern over internet chat rooms and the potential dangers they pose for children. These are places on the web where people can swap messages almost instantaneously with other people in the 'room'. You can either talk to everyone publicly or switch to one-to-one chat mode with anyone in the room. They're immensely popular and mostly harmless fun. A Home Office report published in March 2001 found that of the five million British children who use the internet, more than one million do so in around 100,000 chat rooms around the world.

But there is very little monitoring or policing of these chat rooms, so youngsters can easily be drawn into conversations of an overtly sexual or offensive nature. And it is very easy for chatters to assume a false identity and tell lies. This has led to notorious cases of paedophiles preying on children and cyber-stalkers harassing people generally.

There has been so much concern about this that the Internet Crime Forum, a group including representatives from the Association of Chief Police Officers, child welfare groups, internet companies and the Home Office, has recommended that protected children-only chat rooms be set up. These would be monitored by specially-trained staff skilled at spotting inappropriate or sexually explicit language. Requests for meetings would also be closely scrutinised and vetted sites would carry recognisable safety 'kitemarks'.

Despite the laudable aims of the Internet Crime Forum, doubts must surely remain about any organisation's ability to police so many messages relayed in real time, although such moves must be viewed as a step in the right direction. For the time being then, parents and teachers should educate children about the potential dangers of chat rooms, much as they would about accepting lifts from strangers.

The following advice applies:

❶ Never give out contact information such as your e-mail address, phone number, home or school address to people in chat rooms.

❷ Never agree to meet someone unless you are absolutely sure who it is.

❸ If you do agree to meet someone, do so accompanied by a responsible adult.

As mentioned elsewhere, the only sure way to protect children is to monitor their internet use completely.

Using computers safely

If you are buying a computer and setting up internet access at home or at school for the first time there are some basic, common sense rules you should follow to make sure kids come to no harm.

❶ Make sure children don't sit too close to the screen as it could strain their eyes after prolonged use. Change the font size on screen to make text easier to read if necessary. You can also change the brightness of the screen image to prevent eye strain.

❷ To prevent back and neck strain ensure that users adopt a good posture while sitting at the keyboard. This means keeping a straight back and positioning the screen so that the head can be kept fairly level with it.

❸ When typing there should be support for the wrists to prevent Repetitive Strain Injury-type problems and hands should be cupped as if playing the piano. RSI cases are on the increase, although there are relatively few involving children.

❹ Establish a family or school code of conduct outlining when and how computers are to be used.

Shopping online

Shopping online is as safe, if not safer, than other forms of shopping, particularly shopping by telephone. There are very few cases of fraud involving stolen credit card details, especially when you consider that there are over 500 million people worldwide with net access nowadays.

Yes, there have been some alarming cases of retail websites being breached by hackers and credit card numbers being publicly posted on the web. But most of the time this kind of stunt is pulled by hackers wanting to show how clever they are and to point out security flaws in retailers' computer systems.

People also forget that the problem of net credit card fraud is not really our problem: it's the card issuers' problem. Nine times out of ten we won't be held liable if fraudulent purchases are made using our card details without our knowledge. So long as we haven't been negligent, our liability is restricted to £50. And in most cases, the card issuer accepts full liability anyway, even if you've shopped at foreign websites. The credit card market is very competitive at the moment. Card issuers don't want to risk losing customers by penalising them for something that wasn't their fault.

Several card issuers now offer fraud guarantees with their cards, promising to stand any loss the customer incurs through fraud on the web. This is a clever marketing gimmick, given the continuing level of concern about security. But there's no real need to get such a card just for this reason. Using a credit card online gives you *increased* protection, but more of that later.

How do I know if a website offers secure payments?

These days you're very unlikely to come across a retailer that doesn't offer secure trading. They realise that people just aren't going to buy from them unless they can convince customers that it is safe. So if they have any sense they'll advertise the safety aspects of their service very loudly. But

> **TIP**
>
> *Look out for a closed padlock or unbroken key symbol on retail sites. This tells you that a site is secure.*

you shouldn't take a website's word for it. Your web browser can tell you a great deal.

When you are in secure mode, you will see a closed padlock at the bottom of your web browser window. You should also see the web address changed to begin **https://** instead of the usual **http://**. When you're not in secure mode, the padlock will be open and the address will revert to its normal state.

Encrypting data takes a lot of computer resources and can slow things down considerably on the web, so when you're just browsing a website you don't want to be in secure mode unless you have to. You only need security when you're about to send personal and sensitive information across the net. So online retailers will often give you the option of switching between secure and insecure mode to help speed up your browsing experience.

It's safer paying by credit card

Despite the security fears about using credit cards online, they actually give you *more* protection, not less. This is because Section 75 of the Consumer Credit Act 1974 states that you have an equal claim against the card issuer if the retailer goes bust or fails to deliver the goods in a satisfactory condition. Providing the value of the transaction is worth at least £100 and not more than £30,000 per item, you're covered. This applies even if you've only used the card to pay a deposit. You can find more information about this on the Office of Fair Trading's website (*see page 267 for the address*). NB: You don't have this protection if you pay using debit or charge cards.

How can I trust an online retailer?

It is very important to check out a retailer's credentials before you buy from it. If you've never heard of the company you need to be extra careful, especially if it's a foreign site. On the web it is very easy for fraudsters to set themselves up as legitimate businesses, then simply take your credit card details and scarper without delivering the goods you ordered. After all, creating a website is a lot easier than setting up a false shop front on the high street.

As well as being on guard against possible fraudsters, you need to be wary of sites that do not maintain high standards when it comes to customer service and security. How do you know that the retailer will process your order accurately and on time? How do you know that your personal details are safe from prying eyes, whether inside or outside the company? The brutal truth is that you don't. You have to satisfy yourself about the genuineness and reliability of websites, and this means checking them out and using your common sense.

Follow these rules and you should be safe:

❶ Never give your plastic card or personal details over the net except via a secure server.

❷ Never write down or disclose passwords, log-in names or Personal Identification Numbers (PINs).

❸ Stick to well-known, well-regarded websites if possible. Ask friends for recommendations.

❹ If you've never heard of a website and you're unsure about it, look for physical address and telephone contact details. Test them to establish that the business really exists. Ask your friends if they've heard of it. If you have any remaining doubts, don't deal with them.

❺ Also check that the web address is exactly right. Fraudsters can sometimes set up virtual copies of well-known brand-name websites. A dot here and a hyphen there can make all the difference. And bear in mind that a **.co.uk** or **.uk** ending doesn't necessarily mean that the site is based in the UK.

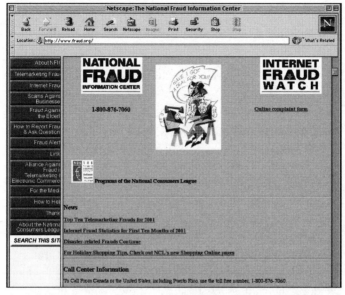

Find out the latest scams and how to protect yourself online with Internet Fraud Watch (www.fraud.org), a US site dedicated to educating consumers.

6 Look for sites that have been given a 'kitemark' certificate by an accreditation scheme, such as TrustUK, VeriSign, or Which? WebTrader.

7 If a web retailer says it belongs to a trade association, check that it really does and find out whether the association operates a code of conduct and any kind of arbitration service should you need to make a complaint.

8 Look for sites that send you an e-mail confirming your order and giving you a unique order number that you can use to track the progress of your purchase. Make sure you keep these e-mails as proof of purchase and for reference if you need to contact the retailer.

9 Ask what delivery guarantees the retailer gives and what its returns policy is. If it is a UK site you're covered by normal consumer law (*see page 263*) and entitled to a full refund if goods are faulty or not as advertised. Be extra vigilant when ordering from abroad because UK law doesn't apply.

❿ If a website is offering something that looks too good to be true, it probably is. Treat with extreme caution. For news on the latest net frauds and scams try sites such as **Internet Fraud Watch** (**www.fraud.org**) and **Internet Scambusters** (**www.scambusters.com**).

⓫ Use a credit card to pay online. The card issuer is obliged to refund you under Section 75 of the Consumer Credit Act if the goods fail to arrive or are damaged (for purchases between £100 and £30,000). There is still a debate within the industry as to whether this law applies to foreign transactions. The Office of Fair Trading thinks it does, the card issuers disagree. At the moment though, they will refund you, but only on a voluntary basis.

Shopping abroad: protecting yourself

As we've pointed out above, there are potential pitfalls buying abroad. So here's a checklist of questions to ask before you flash the plastic:

● Does the retailer deliver internationally?
● Is the item UK-compatible?
● Have you worked out all the costs?
● Does the item have a guarantee?
● Can you trust the retailer?
● Do you know where the retailer is based?
● Does the site offer secure ordering?

Sorting out problems

Buying abroad is fine when things go right – you can net
yourself a bargain. But if things turn nasty, getting them

sorted out can be a real headache. Language barriers, distance and different consumer protection laws can complicate procedures to the extent that you feel like giving up.

If you are unhappy with the service you've received, complain first to the retailer and keep copies of all your correspondence. If this gets you nowhere, you can turn to the following organisations for help:

National Association of Citizens' Advice Bureaux
www.nacab.org.uk
International Marketing Supervision Network
www.imsnricc.org
The European Advertising Standards Alliance
www.easa-alliance.org

Legal action

Only consider legal action as a very last resort. The rules are extremely complicated and you are unlikely to get your legal fees back even if you win your case. For more information on your rights in this area, go to the online shopping advice section of the OFT's website.

Your rights under the law

As far as UK law and the regulators are concerned, there's no difference between shopping online and shopping by mail order or in the high street. UK consumer protection law applies equally well. This states that goods must be:

- as described on the website

- of satisfactory quality

- fit for their purpose

This is why it's important to make records of your transactions. Print off web pages containing product particulars so you have something to refer to when the product arrives. Keep any e-mails, too. If you're not happy, you must have evidence to show that the retailer was in breach of the law as summarised above. If a retailer had pointed out a defect, say, and you hadn't noticed the warning on the website, you would forfeit your right to compensation.

These consumer rights also apply to goods in sales. The retailer is obliged to offer you a full refund if the product doesn't come up to scratch.

Of course, if you just change your mind after pressing the 'Buy Now!' button, or you decide you don't like your purchase when it arrives, you'll have a hard time getting your money back. Having said that, many retailers do operate a 'good will' policy, and offer refunds or exchanges even when they don't have to under the law. It's a good idea to find out whether the online retailer does operate such a policy before you buy online. Some shoppers may feel that it's worth paying a little extra for something at a particular site they know won't cause a fuss if they need to return it for whatever reason. Members of the Direct Marketing Association allow customers to return goods within seven days.

If you're not happy . . .

The same consumer principles apply to online shopping as apply to ordinary shopping. If the goods you buy online are faulty, or not what you thought you ordered, you must tell the retailer as soon as possible. A long delay can work in the retailer's favour if a dispute arises – it can be interpreted as acceptance on your part. It also gives weight to the retailer's potential argument that you must have damaged the item yourself and you just want to get your money back unfairly. Prompt action gives slippery retailers far less room for manoeuvre.

One of the many advantages of e-mail is that you can complain very quickly. It's also easy to keep copies of correspondence, unlike telephone calls. Keeping receipts is obviously a good idea also.

Don't be put off if a retailer tries to escape its obligations. It can't just pass the buck and blame the manufacturer. If the goods come with a manufacturer's guarantee, though, it may be sensible to send off the registration card. Sometimes you get extra protection.

You are normally obliged to accept a retailer's offer to mend the goods if they are faulty, but you're under no pressure to accept them if the repairs don't work. You can still ask for compensation, although technically you're thought to have 'accepted' the goods by then. And bear in mind that just because goods are in a sale, it doesn't mean the retailer is not responsible if they turn out to be dodgy. You should expect some wear and tear on second-hand goods, but they should still comply with the main principles listed above.

Who to complain to ...

If you don't get anywhere with the retailer and you're still dissatisfied, there are a number of bodies you can complain to. A list of useful web addresses is given on page xx. The relevant organisation will depend largely on the type of complaint.

For example, the retailer may belong to a trade association that has a code of practice for its members. If the web company is in breach of the code, the association should take up the case on your behalf. Some associations operate low-cost arbitration services to sort out disputes between customers and their members. The existence of a code of practice also helps other bodies judge whether the member company has been acting unfairly or unlawfully.

Alternatively, you could seek advice from a **Citizens' Advice Bureau** or from **Trading Standards** departments. Trading standards departments have powers to investigate complaints about false or misleading descriptions or prices, and the safety of consumer goods (except in Northern Ireland). They will often advise on everyday shopping problems and are usually all too aware of unreliable or troublesome retailers. If you're not sure about a particular website, it may be an idea to ring a trading standards office first, to see if they've had any complaints about it.

You can also seek the advice of a solicitor – some working in law centres or advice agencies will offer advice for free. Your local Citizens' Advice Bureau can help you find a low-cost or free solicitor. As a last resort, you could take the retailer to court, although this can be expensive and time-consuming.

If your complaint is about the way something is being advertised on the web, go to the **Advertising Standards Authority**. The ASA is responsible for enforcing British Codes of Advertising and Sales Promotion, whether the ads are on the TV, in newspapers or on the net. Ads must be legal, decent, honest and truthful.

The ASA code states that you are entitled to a full refund if you return the goods within seven days of receiving them. And you don't have to pay if they've taken so long to arrive that you don't want them any more. The standard time limit for deliveries is 30 days.

E-mail is often used for direct marketing purposes and many of the companies that advertise this way belong to the **Direct Marketing Association**. The DMA has an independent adjudication service to help in disputes between customers and member firms. It also offers a useful e-mail privacy protection service (*see Privacy, page 241*).

Useful web addresses

Office of Fair Trading	**www.oft.gov.uk**
Trading Standards Office	**www.tradingstandards.gov.uk**
Northern Ireland Trading Standards	**www.tssni.gov.uk**
National Association of Citizens' Advice Bureaux	**www.nacab.org.uk**
Advertising Standards Authority	**www.asa.org.uk**
Direct Marketing Association	**www.dma.org.uk**
Data Protection Registrar	**www.dpr.gov.uk**
E-mail Preference Service	**www.emailpreference service.co.uk**
TrustUK	**www.trustuk.org.uk**
Which? WebTrader Scheme	**www.which.net/webtrader/ index.html**
Interactive Media in Retail Group	**www.imrg.org**

Buying from individuals

When you buy something from a private individual, through a classified ads website, for example, you're much less protected. The old rule – 'caveat emptor' – applies. But the goods still must be 'as described'. So if someone is selling a car and describes it as 'in pristine condition' and you discover that it's a rust-bucket, you're entitled to a refund. In practice, this can be difficult to enforce. For this reason, some unscrupulous retailers pose as private sellers to flog off substandard goods in a less regulated environment.

Protecting yourself at online auctions

When buying at auction you also have fewer statutory rights than you do when buying from an ordinary online retailer.

Although public pressure has often led to the removal of auction items considered dangerous, illegal or offensive, this is still some way from the auctioneer accepting full responsibility for the items it does allow on its site.

If the seller is another retailer, the terms of the contract will still be subject to the test of fairness set out in the Unfair Terms in Consumer Contracts Regulations 1994. But this doesn't apply to private sellers. So look especially closely at the site's terms and conditions for any mention of guarantees and for information on what to do if you want to make a complaint.

Also bear in mind that online auction sites are not infallible. The systems they operate are complex and can go wrong from time to time. So it's important that you keep records of the bidding process. For example, you should print off pages at crucial stages, such as when the reserve has been met, and when you've been successful in your bid. The last thing you want is an e-mail from the auction site telling you you've bought something completely different at a price you cannot afford. This has happened before, so it's as well to have evidence to hand if you need to prove your case in a dispute. Also, keep all e-mails you send to and receive from the auction site.

For high-value items an 'escrow' service is a good idea. This involves a 'trusted third party' acting as an intermediary between buyer and seller. Once a buyer has placed a successful bid, he or she sends the money to the escrow service. Once the money has been received, the seller is given word that it's safe to ship the goods. The funds are not released to the seller until the buyer has received the goods and is happy with them.

The main advantage of this system is that both buyer and seller have to sign up to it. A fraudster who has no intention of delivering the goods is obviously thwarted. So if a seller refuses to sign up to an escrow service, alarm bells should begin ringing in bidders' ears.

Here's a list of safety tips:

❶ Find out as much about the seller as possible and stick to those with very high approval ratings from other auction site members.

❷ Always pay by credit card if possible and be very wary of 'cash only' offers.

❸ Be sceptical about over-enthusiastic product descriptions and claims about originality and rarity. How can you be sure the item is really in 'mint condition' or isn't a forgery?

❹ If something is being offered at a knock-down price that you know is worth a lot more, ask yourself why. Has it been stolen?

❺ For expensive items, use an escrow service to protect yourself against the goods arriving in an unsatisfactory condition or not being delivered at all.

❻ Be wary of sellers with anonymous web-based e-mail addresses, as opposed to traceable addresses provided by internet service providers. There may be a reason why the seller wants to hide his identity.

❼ Don't get carried away bidding and end up paying too much for something. You may be the victim of a 'shill bidding' scam.

Financial Protection

The Financial Services and Markets Act 2000 finally came into force on 1 December 2001. Brokers and other investment firms that were regulated by the Securities and Futures Authority are now regulated by the Financial Services Authority (**www.fsa.gov.uk**), the unified regulator for the whole financial services industry.

The FSA has four main aims:

● maintaining confidence in the UK financial system

● promoting public understanding of the financial system

● securing the right degree of protection for consumers

● contributing to reduce financial crime

New complaints procedure

A new complaints procedure is now in force. If you have a complaint against a broker or any other investment-related company you have to approach them first and give them an opportunity to sort things out. If you remain dissatisfied, you can contact the **Financial Ombudsman Scheme** (**www.financial-ombudsman.org.uk**).

The new Ombudsman scheme will bring together the eight existing dispute-resolution schemes covering financial services. All the current schemes to be replaced by the FOS will operate under the day-to-day management of the FOS and are based at:

Financial Ombudsman Scheme
South Quay Plaza
183 Marsh Wall
London
E14 9SR

The unified Ombudsman is empowered to make binding decisions based on what is 'fair and reasonable'. This means there is no longer any separate arbitration option available, but you are free to take the matter to court if you still feel hard done by. The service is available to private individuals and businesses with an annual turnover of less than £1 million.

There is an excellent comprehensive step-by-step section, 'How to complain', on the FOS website. It is well worth a read – forewarned is forearmed!

New compensation scheme

The FSA has also set up a new compensation scheme that is the responsibility of the **Financial Services Compensation Scheme Ltd.** (FSCS – www.fscs.org.uk). It can pay compensation to eligible consumers if any of its member firms breaks the rules. The compensation limits are:

Deposits – maximum £31,700 (100% of £2,000 and 90% of the next £33,000)

Investments – covering when an authorised investment company goes bust, taking your money and investments with it, and when you lose out through poor investment advice or bad investment management: maximum £48,000 (100% of £30,000 and 90% of the next £20,000).

The money that is used to pay compensation comes from charges levied on authorised firms. There is no charge to investors who claim on the FSCS and you don't need legal or professional advice to make a claim.

Who's in charge of the net?

Well, no-one really. For the purists out there, that's its beauty. It embodies the principles of free speech in their purest form. For others, it appears to be a chaotic nightmare, a haven for the depraved and the psychopathic. The techies who charted the net's rise from humble, innocent beginnings in the seventies, see the rise of rampant commercialism on the web as a sad diminution of its ethos of free exchange. In the US, home to the world's most dedicated conspiracy theorists, the net is often portrayed as the last truly free place on earth, in an age increasingly dominated by governmental and commercial surveillance of all aspects of our lives.

In many ways it is a strong force for democracy and freedom of expression. Tibetan monks, persecuted by Chinese occupying forces, have often used the net to communicate with the rest of the world, as have other downtrodden minorities. As a breathtakingly powerful tool for mass communication, the net can empower people by giving them information that they may not have been able to get hold of before. More than any other technological development it has shown that information is power.

So the net is still largely self-regulating, with businesses and service providers working out amongst themselves how best to deal with problems of security and authenticity. Governmental interference is not welcomed by the net industry, but the need for businesses to find common security standards to facilitate e-commerce has led to an inevitable increase in the part that governments have to play. The web is transforming economies now, not just helping academics to swap ideas.

There is a constant battle between the libertarians and those who would regulate the net far more tightly, citing the ubiquity of pornography and other obscene or anti-social content to bolster their case. The problem is that as the net expands to become a global phenomenon, reaching Communist countries as well, Western ideas concerning freedom of speech don't go down too well.

Generally, governments have been happy to sit and watch developments, seeing how far existing legislation can be stretched to cover online activities. For the most part, the web is just another publishing medium. So existing laws to do with libel, for example, apply equally online as offline. But there are some unique problems, many of them to do with copyright. The web has made it very easy to copy and distribute images and sound in clear breach of copyright law. The demise of the US music file sharing company, Napster, is a case in point. Yet the net industry still believes technology will find solutions to these problems without the need for governments to impose cumbersome laws and potentially stifle business.

It is in the area of security that governments have made their presence felt. Law enforcement agencies generally want to retain the ability to open encrypted mail and get behind security firewalls when necessary in the name of national security. Civil libertarians argue that such powers would be open to too much abuse. Other commentators believe that try as it might, the government simply won't be able to control encryption because the technology is already out there and well-established. Although the US tried to restrict the international use of 128-bit encryption to financial services, it eventually had to give up trying to control its use. The cat was let out of the bag a long time ago.

Glossary

ADSL – Asynchronous Digital Subscriber Line – a way of sending digital data over the conventional telephone network at speeds up to 40 times faster than the fastest modem. Downloading data is faster than uploading.

aggregator – website that brings together in one place lots of links to other websites. It may offer its own entertainment, information and shopping services, too.

applet – a small helper program (usually written in Java programming language) that is downloaded from the net into your Web browser as and when necessary.

backbone – high capacity data motorways that link other networks together.

bandwidth – the speed with which data can be sent across the network. The bigger the bandwidth the more data can be sent at one time and so the faster the system.

banner ad – graphical link on a web page usually advertising a commercial service.

BBS – Bulletin Board System. A system that allows you to post and receive messages and download files.

beta programs – usually free pilot software programs released to the public by software companies for testing and evaluation purposes.

bits – the smallest pieces of information a computer deals with.

bits per second (bps) – the standard measure of speed in transmitting data. A modem with a speed of 56 kilobits per second can download data at up to 56,000 bits per second, though it rarely achieves such maximum performance.

byte – a piece of digital information containing eight bits.

Boolean operators – words such as AND, NOT, OR which help you be more specific when using a search engine.

broadband services – high-speed connections to the internet, 10 to 100 times faster than the fastest modem.

browser – software program, such as Netscape Navigator or Internet Explorer that helps you surf the World Wide Web.

cable modem – a gizmo that connects your computer to a fibre optic cable as opposed to the usual twisted copper wires of the conventional telephone network.

CD-ROM – compact disk read-only memory. A disk that can store large amounts of information.

channels – another word for web services usually incorporated into web browsers, portal sites and search engines.

chat room – forum for sending and receiving instantaneous messages to any number of other people who are joining the 'conversation'.

click through – the process of clicking on a link or advert on a web page and going to another site.

client – another name for a helper software program, such as a web browser or FTP manager.

compressed file – a file that has been crunched down to take up less memory so that you can download it quicker. To read these files you need to decompress them using a program such as WinZip.

cookie – a small file downloaded on to your computer that enables a web company to track where you've been on the net.

cyberspace – abstract description of the world of the net and the web.

digital signature – a way of authenticating the origin and authorship of digital documents.

directory – a categorised list of links to websites.

Domain Name System (DNS) – the way of translating domain names, such as 'Excite.com', into Internet Protocol addresses that identify individual computers by a unique series of numbers. These domain names are managed and distributed by 'nameservers'.

download – transfer files and web pages on to your computer.

dynamic IP – an internet protocol address for your computer that changes every time you go online, helping to prevent websites identifying you as a repeat visitor. Not all ISPs support dynamic IP.

e-mail – electronic mail. Messages that can be sent from one computer to another using a unique address. You can also attach files to your messages.

encryption – a way of jumbling up digital data so that it cannot be read by anyone who does not have the key to unscramble the message.

File Transfer Protocol (FTP) – standard for transferring files across the net.

FAQ – frequently asked questions. A document on a website or newsgroup that answers common queries.

firewall – a security system that prevents outsiders gaining access to a particular network of computers.

fix or **patch** – extra code added to a software programs to improve it or iron out a glitch

flaming – sending abusive messages via e-mail or a newsgroup.

forwarding service – e-mail server that will redirect mail sent to one address to another address of your choice.

freeware – software that you can download for free.

Gigabyte (Gbyte) – unit of measurement for computer memory, roughly one billion bytes.

hit – a file found as a result of search request.

home page – normally the first page you see when accessing a website.

host – any computer open to external online access, usually providing services for other computers. Also known as a server.

HTML – HyperText Mark-up Language. The standard language for displaying text in web pages.

HTML editor – software that helps you translate standard word processing text into HTML code for web pages.

HTTP – HyperText Transfer Protocol. The standard for transferring HTML documents across the net. Web addresses always begin with the letters http.

HyperText – text or graphics that when clicked on take you to another site called a hyperlink.

Internet Protocol (IP) address – a unique address assigned to every computer on the net that usually consists of four sets of numbers separated by dots.

ISDN – Integrated Services Digital Network. A way of transferring digital data over standard telephone wires that gets rid of the need for modems. Can achieve speeds of up to 128Kbps.

ISP – Internet Service Provider.

leased line – permanent and dedicated high-speed connection to the internet (2Mbps usually), mostly adopted by businesses.

mailer – another word for e-mail software.

mailing list – service that delivers information or news to subscribers via e-mail.

Messenger – Netscape's e-mail program that comes with the Navigator web browser.

Megabyte (MB) – a million bytes.

meta-search engine – search engine that trawls several other search engines as well as its own database for a more comprehensive search.

modem – gizmo for translating digital data into analogue format for transfer over the telephone lines.

multimedia – the integration of sound, text, pictures and video in digital communication.

Navigator – another word for browser, but usually shorthand for Netscape Navigator, the second most popular browser.

net – short for internet.

netiquette – code of behaviour for net surfers whilst online.

newsgroup – a particular discussion group where people can read and post messages on a specific topic. The biggest collection of such newsgroups is Usenet.

newsreader – browser for reading and organizing Usenet messages.

notifier – web service that will e-mail you when a particular web page you're interested in is updated or changed.

offline – not connected to the net.

online – connected to the net.

Outlook Express – a Microsoft e-mail program that comes with its Internet Explorer web browser.

PDF files – files created using Adobe Acrobat that require Acrobat Reader to view them.

plug-in – an additional program downloaded on to your web browser that allows you to watch a video, for example, or listen to live radio.

portal – a general-purpose website that may contain its own entertainment and information services as well as links to many others. It usually incorporates a search engine or directory.

ripper – a program that transfers music from a CD onto your hard drive.

search engine – a program that interrogates the net for files or web pages containing or relating to words or phrases you enter into the search box.

Secure Sockets Layer (SSL) – system developed by Netscape for encrypting online payment details.

server – *see* host

shareware – software that is usually free for an evaluation period, after which you have to pay a registration fee.

signature file – a file usually containing your contact details that you can include automatically with your e-mails.

SMTP – Simple Mail Transfer Protocol. The standard for sending e-mail across the net.

spam – unsolicited e-mail.

streaming audio and video – listening to music and radio, or watching video, while the data is in the process of being downloaded, rather than having to wait for entire files to be downloaded first.

surfing – exploring files on the net.

tags – instructions on how to format text and images in HTML for web pages.

TCP/IP – Transport Control Protocol/Internet Protocol – the standard way computers talk to each other on the internet.

thread – a discussion within a Usenet discussion group.

traffic – the term used for the flow of visits sites receive from browsing surfers.

upload – transfer files, documents and web pages from your computer on to the net.

URL – Uniform Resource Locator. The standard way of identifying any service on the net, such as
http://www.sunday-times.co.uk

Usenet – the collective name for discussion newsgroups on the internet.

vCard – Netscape Messenger's name for a signature file.

virus – a computer program designed to corrupt information on another computer.

web hosting service – company that will store and maintain websites on their own servers, register domain names, and offer other services, such as e-mail and URL forwarding.

web server – computer that stores web pages that can be accessed by other computers.

Wireless Application Protocol (WAP) – standard for making web pages suitable for viewing on hand-held devices, such as mobile phones, pagers and personal organizers.

World Wide Web (the web, or www) – collective name for all documents on the Net written in HTML that can be read using a web browser.

zip – to compress data so that it takes up less space and can be downloaded faster. Once received, zipped files need to be unzipped by a software program or else they can't be read.

285